Real Estate
Model Letter Desk Book

Morrie Kirby

Prentice-Hall, Inc.   Englewood Cliffs, New Jersey

Prentice-Hall International, Inc., *London*
Prentice-Hall of Australia, Pty. Ltd., *Sydney*
Prentice-Hall of Canada, Ltd., *Toronto*
Prentice-Hall of India Private Ltd., *New Delhi*
Prentice-Hall of Japan, Inc., *Tokyo*
Prentice-Hall of Southeast Asia Pte. Ltd., *Singapore*
Whitehall Books, Ltd., *Wellington, New Zealand*

© 1978 by

Prentice-Hall, Inc.
Englewood Cliffs, N.J.

Third Printing . . . . . April, 1981

Library of Congress Cataloging in Publication Data

Kirby, Morrie.
    Real estate model letter desk book.

    1. Real estate business--Records and correspondence.
2. Commercial correspondence. I. Title.
HF5734.R3K57   658'.91'33333   77-17832
ISBN 0-13-764316-0

Printed in the United States of America

ABOUT THE AUTHOR . . .

Maurice (Morrie) W. Kirby is presently Vice-President of CENTURY 21 Kirby-Yowell, Realtors, in Omaha, Nebraska. He has been in the real estate business since 1958 and holds G.R.I. and C.R.B. designations. Mr. Kirby has been active in his local, state and national real estate associations. He has served on five committees on the local level, and for three years served as a Director for the Multiple Listing Service of the Omaha Board of Realtors. He chaired the Education and Grievance Committees. He also has served as an instructor for the Board's Orientation and Indoctrination sessions.

He has taught the pre-license course for the Nebraska Realtor's Association and was state chairman for the National Institution of Real Estate Brokers in Nebraska in 1974.

He has also taught *Real Estate Salesmanship and Brokerage* at the University of Nebraska at Omaha for the past two years. He holds a Bachelor of Science Degree from Creighton University in Omaha, Nebraska, and a Master of Arts Degree from Nebraska University in Lincoln, Nebraska.

Mr. Kirby is a past president of the West Suburban Optimist Club, and has served on a school board and various community boards. In addition, in 1976 Mr. Kirby was elected "Realtor of the Year" by the Omaha Board of Realtors.

WHAT THIS BOOK WILL DO FOR YOU

At this moment you may have a letter that you, if given a choice, would rather not have to write. But you must write it. How many minutes or hours will you needlessly spend wondering what you are going to say to that certain client or that troublesome sales associate? How much time will you waste thinking about all those letter-writing situations that demand action now?

In real estate, time is money. Think of how much more productive you could be if you had practical assistance that could save you time, allow you to get a message across in a clear and concise manner and obtain the desired results.

You have that aid in your hands—a reference tool that will allow you to accomplish these three objectives. It will assist you in getting your message across to clients, your sales associates, mortgage officers, attorneys, and the many other people with whom you work in the real estate profession. It will provide for you that extra assistance that will stimulate people to action even though you may be miles apart. And, on top of it all, it will save you much valuable time.

This book contains over 250 tested and successful real estate model letters. Whenever you are faced with the task of writing a tough-to-write letter, all you have to do is turn to the Table of Contents, select the model letter that applies to your specific situation, then dictate it to your secretary. It is that easy.

In many instances, the letters reproduced within these pages can be used with a minimum of changes. Some will require no revisions at all to meet your needs.

This book puts at your fingertips the successful letter-writing

experience of dozens of sales associates and sales managers from across the country. You'll never again waste time and effort composing an effective letter. These model letters cover almost every conceivable situation, occasion and circumstance: you'll find "know how" letters for sales associates, model letters to listing and selling clients, letters to awaken lagging sales associates, letters that turn complaints into compliments, model letters for improving public relations . . . and hundreds of others.

Have you ever spent hours trying to find just the right words to use in obtaining a price adjustment on a listing that isn't selling? Chapter 4 will really make it easy for you. How would you like follow-up letters to purchasing clients that will obtain more sales for you? Chapter 6 will help you do just that!

All the tough letter-writing situations are covered. Do you have to write a tenant for overdue rent? Go quickly to Chapter 7. Do you have to get tough during a loan procedure? See Chapter 11.

You will also find in this book hundreds of ideas that will make your every day letter more productive. Do you ever see sales associates troubled during a tight money market? A model letter in Chapter 13 will help keep them on the track. Did you ever have a seller take items from a home that he or she shouldn't have taken? See Chapter 14.

What about that letter to congratulate a friend without sounding too flowery or phony? See Chapter 9.

A poor letter can cost you sales. A letter written carelessly can lose a sales associate or cause him or her to have problems with their clients. Could your letters be causing problems for your sales associates? Dissatisfaction among your clients? Look at a recent letter you wrote and compare it to what you find in this book under the appropriate heading. The difference you see is what sets this book apart and makes it a valuable reference tool that you will want to keep on your desk at all times.

The letters provided in this book have produced favorable results for others. They can do the same for you. One sales manager submitted a sales associate listing letter to me and acknowledged at the bottom that many members of his staff quickly became better listors through the use of this letter. Other contributors reported that their letters had made such favorable impressions on clients that they either called stating what a fine letter they had received or returned the letter with favorable comments at the bottom. The letters that reached this book won their way in by being practical, tested and proven letters. The contributing sales associates and sales managers who share these letters with you do so because they are proud of them and very proud of the results they have obtained. These letters come from small, medium and large-size real estate offices from across the country. They will fit the needs of any size organization.

These letters are not theoretical in any way. They are the actual correspondence used today by sales managers and sales associates involved in the very practical world of real estate selling.

Writing a good letter can be a tedious, painstaking experience for many of us. My purpose in this book is to take a hard job and make it easier for you. A real estate salesperson makes money by seeing and selling people. It is a numbers game—the more people you see, the greater the chance of making more sales. So, I am giving you an opportunity to cut down on some of the necessary but time-consuming details of salesmanship—one of these being effective letter-writing.

It costs you no more money to write and send a good business letter than a poor one. With good models to follow, you will save time and make money. Other people have done the hard work of writing these letters. You can use these models and reap the benefits. You will find this book and the letters in it to be functional, practical and a valuable reference tool that will save you much time and effort and improve your letter-writing results.

Morrie Kirby

ACKNOWLEDGMENTS

Many Realtors, real estate agents and individuals in related fields took the time and effort to respond to my requests for letters that would serve as models for their colleagues. I owe sincere thanks to and gratefully acknowledge the assistance given to me by the following people. Included in this list are three fine secretaries and my wife, who gave helpful suggestions and hours of devoted typing. Thanks again to . . .

R. H. Abernathy, Jr., N. P. Dodge Co., Realtors, Omaha, Nebraska
John Abraham, C.R.B., Abraham Realty, Co., Adrian, Michigan
William E. Barnett, C.R.B., Barnett, Realtors, Wenatchee, Washington
William Barrett, C.R.B., Barrett-Housel & Associates, Inc., Lexington, Nebraska
H. L. "Sam" Bass, C.R.B., Professional Real Estate, Inc., Baltimore, Maryland
Lewis Bass, C.R.B., Bass & Weisberg, Realtors, Louisville, Kentucky
Dorothy R. Bates, C.R.B., Dorothy R. Bates, Inc., Wilton, Connecticut
Richard E. Beaty, C.R.B., Beaty Associates, Huntington, Indiana
Frank J. Boblak, C.R.B., F. J. Boblak and Associates, Oak Lawn, Illinois
Herman Brown, C.R.B., Herman Brown Real Estate & Insurance, Inc., Alexandria, Indiana
Frank A. Burgdorf, C.R.B., John H. Bollin & Co., Columbia, South Carolina
H. Harland Crowell, Jr., C.R.B., Crowell & Co., Inc., McLean, Virginia
William B. Craig, Attorney-at-Law, Omaha, Nebraska
Judith E. Dellorte, C.R.B., Continental Real Estate, South, Chicago Heights, Illinois
Annette Dundee, Closing Secretary, Ball Real Estate, Omaha, Nebraska
Beverly J. Eastberg, Secretary, Ball Real Estate, Omaha, Nebraska
John B. Effrein, G.R.I., N.B.C., Realtors, Omaha, Nebraska
William A. Eyth, C.R.B., William A. Eyth, Realtors, Beatrice, Nebraska
Roy Fair, C.R.B., Fair Realty, Inc., Aurora, Illinois

Shirley Feagins, Secretary, Ball Real Estate, Omaha, Nebraska

Jack L. Gale, C.R.B., Gale Associates, Inc., Realtors, Maitland, Florida

Lanny A. Gardner, C.R.B., Gardner, Co., Realtors, Oklahoma City, Oklahoma

Gene F. Girard, C.R.B., Girard Realty, Inc., Schenectady, New York

Lou Goldman, C.R.B., Goldman Associates, Realtors, Daytona Beach, Florida

Arnold Goldsborough, C.R.B., Goldsborough, Co., Realtors, Wilmington, Delaware

Lavina Goracke, Sales Associate, Ball Real Estate, Omaha, Nebraska

Therese Haller, G.R.I., Ball Real Estate, Omaha, Nebraska

C. J. Harris, C.R.B., Harris-Hanby, Realtors, Wilmington, Delaware

Galen L. Hauger, Hauger-Bunch, Inc., Lakeland, Florida

Bob Jones, C.R.B., Bob Jones, Realtor, San Antonio, Texas

Vic Karels, C.R.B., Fowler Real Estate and Insurance, Inc., Realtors, Boulder, Colorado

Clyde A. Kautz, C.R.B., Kautz and Co., Realtors, Glen Ellyn, Illinois

Rubin and Shirley Kichen, Wagner Realty, Scottsdale, Arizona

Kimball Foundation, Edward Kramer, Founder, St Louis, Missouri

Cecelia A. Kirby, My Dear Wife, Omaha, Nebraska

Beatrice A. Marshall, C.R.B., Beatrice A. Marshall, Realtor, Wayne, Pennsylvania

Ed McGill, C.M.H., Realtors, Omaha, Nebraska

Donald A. Nielsen, P.H.D., Program Chairman Real Estate and Land-Use Economics, University of Nebraska at Omaha, Omaha, Nebraska

Sam M. Nein, Nein and Co., Realtors, Boulder, Colorado

Dan Nuttle, C.R.B., R.J. Den Herder Co., Jackson, Michigan

Vince Penza, C.R.B., Vince Penza, Realtor, Jacksonville, Illinois

Rich Port, C.R.B., Rich Port, Realtor, La Grange, Illinois

Gary Prichard, C.R.B., Compass Realty, Inc., Tacoma, Washington

Roy J. Riley, C.R.B., Crown Realty, Co., Des Moines, Iowa

Andrew G. C. Sage, II, Sage Land Development Co., Inc., Jackson, Wyoming

Elaine Schiff, C.R.B., Elaine Schiff, Realtors, Louisville, Kentucky

James B. Schomacker, C.R.B., The Gooding, Co., Lima, Ohio

T. G. Slappey, Jr., C.R.B., Slappey Realty Company, Albany, Georgia

Dick Sowash, C.R.B., Century 21, Dick Sowash, Realtors, Anderson, Indiana

W. E. Stuht, Maenner, Realtors, Omaha, Nebraska

Myron Tarnoff, Sales Executive, Omaha, Nebraska

Harold G. Trimble, Jr., C.R.E., Harold G. Trimble and Associates, San Francisco, California

Robert M. Yaguda, C.R.B., Cohn-Yaguda-Cronin Realty, Inc., Albany, New York

Ralph F. Yaeger, C.R.B., Cline, Realtors, Cincinnati, Ohio

Conrad S. Young, President, United of Omaha, Omaha, Nebraska

James M. Yowell, C.R.B., President Ball Real Estate, Omaha, Nebraska

TABLE OF CONTENTS

Chapter 4

Dealing With the Seller During and After
the Sale With Proven Letters – 66

Chapter 5

Model Letters That Get Potential Real Estate
Buyers Ready to Buy – 106

Chapter 6

Following Up On Buyers: Model Letters
That Can Get You More Sales – 122

Chapter 7

Model Letters to Real Estate
Lessees and Lessors – 148

Chapter 8

How to Use Letters to Make More
Sales to Real Estate Investors – 180

Chapter 9

Effective Publicity and Public
Relations Letters – 199

Chapter 10

Model Letters That Present Real Estate
Appraisal Information Effectively – 225

Chapter 11

Model Letters for Dealing With Banks and Other Financial Institutions – 249

Chapter 12

Dealing With Legal Problems and Attorneys Through Effective Model Letters – 268

Chapter 13

Model Letters That Motivate Real Estate Salesmen To Sell – 285

Chapter 14

Letters That Can Settle Disputes
Quickly and Effectively – 310

Chapter 1

Model Letters for Counselling
Potential Real Estate Sellers

This chapter provides 13 model letters you can use to advise and counsel prospective sellers of real estate, including . . .

15

1-1   MODEL LETTER ADVISING SELLER TO DELAY THE SALE OF A HOME

Dear _____:

I received your letter last Wednesday and it was certainly nice hearing from you. It sounds as though you and your family thoroughly enjoy Arizona.

As you requested, two of my sales associates and I thoroughly examined your property. You have a fine home in an excellent location. Also it seems you have chosen a good tenant.

After completing the <u>Competitive Market Analysis,</u> it is my opinion that your property should sell in the range of $21,000 to $22,000.

I am sure you will agree that the price is right, but I recommend that you wait until after the first of the year to sell your property. I make this statement because of the tight money situation at the present time. The discount points are extremely high to the seller when he sells on no-down or minimum-down financing—V.A. or F.H.A. I mention these two types of loans because a majority of homes are sold through these avenues of financing. The discount points today to the seller on these loans range from 12% to 16%.

In simple terms, this means if you sold your property for $22,000, and the purchaser obtained a 100% loan, you as a seller would pay between $2,640.00 to $3,520.00 to the mortgage company for the purchaser to get the loan. In my opinion, this is too high and I feel this situation will change drastically after the first of the year. Many mortgage loan officers think that the points to the seller at the beginning of next year should range between 3% and 6%.

Your property has certainly appreciated in value from the time you purchased it, but why should you lose much of this appreciation because of the point system?

If you must sell at this time, please call me and we will discuss the total mortgage situation more thoroughly. If you can wait three or four months, it would be prudent to do so. I will contact you in January concerning the money situation at that time.

Thank you again for remembering me, and keep me posted on your thinking.

Your friend,

1-2   BEING CANDID IN COUNSELLING A PROSPECTIVE SELLER

Dear _____:

Thank you for your letter of January 22, 19__. Your mother and I examined your property at __ _____ Avenue on January 25, 19__.

I will answer your questions in the order you asked them:

1. If you were to keep the property for the rental income, I feel the following repairs would be necessary:
   A. Paint outside of house and garage.
   B. City code requires 100 amp. electrical service; you now have 60 amp. service. This would have to be corrected. Also city code requires an inspection of the plumbing, heating and roofing. City inspectors are checking all older properties. The heating plant appears good; I can't tell about the plumbing or roofing. Repairs may be needed.
2. The reasonable rental rate of the property is $80.00 per month.
3. If the property were to be sold:
   A. The reasonable market value would be approximately $8,000. I used 6 similar homes in the area of your house for comparison. The buyer, as you know, eventually sets the price.
   B. I would say that there is a buyer, but it will be a tough job of selling. The 235 program is no more for at least 18 months.
   C. We would be glad to handle the listing. Our fee is 7% or a minimum commission of $900.00.
   D. The expenses involved would be the following—these figures are approximate:

Examination of abstract	$ 35.00
State Documentary Stamps	8.80
Seller's Loan Discount	400.00
(5% of the loan $8,000)	
Repairs, Painting & Inspections	1,300.00
(painting, electrical, plumbing,	
and city code)	

Commission 900.00
Buyer's Closing Costs 400.00
(this kind of property draws the
buyer with no money)   _____
(approx.) $3,043.80

4. Concerning investing in other real estate:
   A. Your return would be much better on two good $15,000–$17,000 properties in good locations rather than on one $30,000 house.
   B. The mortgage terms would be 20% initial investment.
   C. The taxes, insurance and normal maintenance on a $15,000 house would be (again, these are approximate):
      Taxes $400.00
      Insurance   50.00
      Maintenance   450.00
      (3% is a good average figure)
   D. A reasonable rental value on a $15,000–$17,000 house is between $165.00–$200.00 per month.
   E. The demand for good rental property in the _____ area is very good.
   F. We can handle the rental and maintenance. Our fees are:
      1.) ½ of the first month's rent for initial fee of renting.
      2.) 7% of the monthly rental or a minimum of $10.00.
      3.) Our fee for maintenance is 10% of what the tradesmen charge.

   Thank you for your trust in our organization, and I hope this letter has answered your questions.

                              Sincerely,

1-3 MODEL LETTER TO PROSPECTIVE SELLER STRESSING THE IMPORTANCE OF PROPER PRICING

Dear _____:

      Planning to sell your home? Here are a dozen reasons why it is so important to price residential property realistically:

1. Overpricing reduces the response the Realtor will receive from his advertising and so reduces the chances of a sale.
2. Your property must compete with similar properties on the market. Buyers shop by comparison—homes not comparing favorably with others the buyers have inspected do not sell.
3. Buyers expect more at a higher price and failing to find all they had hoped for at that price become disinterested.
4. Most overpriced homes remain unsold for too long a time. Buyers aware of this long period of exposure are hesitant to buy—fearful that there is something wrong with the home. This increased resistance makes a sale very difficult.
5. Agents tend to lose their enthusiasm for a home after a number of unfavorable reactions from buyers. Many of them discontinue showing the property.
6. No Realtor makes a practice of taking overpriced listings and having his "for sale" signs on the property for months without results. He does not want to become known as a poor merchandiser.
7. A real estate salesman's most precious commodity is his TIME. Therefore, he cannot afford to spend his time working on overpriced listings.
8. Overpricing tends to force buyers who could purchase in your area to look elsewhere.
9. The right price is of the utmost importance in the sale of any commodity. Homes priced right usually sell after a normal market exposure.
10. The Realtor will fail to provide the seller with real service if the home is not listed at a realistic price. It is difficult for a

Realtor to build his business if he has many disgruntled sellers with unsold properties. Therefore, he avoids taking over-priced houses.

11. Many times overpricing causes a substantial monetary loss because the owner is compelled to own two homes. Some of these double costs are taxes, insurance, maintenance, heat, interest on equity, etc. These expenses are then combined with the many inconveniences the seller encounters.

12. Overpricing accomplishes nothing because most homes sell for their fair market value. The advantages of realistic pricing far outweigh any consideration to price a property more than 5–10% above the fair market value.

Yours very truly,

1-4   HOW TO STRESS THE IMPORTANCE OF AN EXCLUSIVE AGENCY

Dear _____:

EXCLUSIVE AGENCY
From the Owner's Standpoint

The exclusive agency listing is the only way a real estate broker can serve his client properly. Would you have ten lawyers represent you in a law suit, each working independently of the other? It is better to be represented by one agent than to be misrepresented by a dozen.

From one agent you have the right to demand proper attention to your property; from a dozen brokers you have no right to expect anything. Why not get the kind of service that is most likely to result in a sale? An agent working only on exclusives can give your property proper attention; can afford to advertise it; and is more likely to effect a sale, and at a better price.

Can you expect a broker to try to get you the best possible price for your property knowing that a dozen others are offering it also? No. He will do what you have forced him to do; sell it if he can, at the price the purchasers offer. If he does not, one of the agents will, and he knows it. If you look to one agent only, you know that he is advertising your property properly—he can offer it freely, in the best channels, and in the best method to attract buyers. You and he would be protected against piracy.

A competent and self-respecting agent would rather list ten properties exclusively than one hundred in the old slipshod manner. If you are one of the ten, your chance of selling, and at a good price, is better than if you are one of the hundred. Some owners fear that an exclusive agency will prevent them from selling their property through some other source. This is a mistake. Any conscientious exclusive agent is willing to serve his client's best interests—even by dividing his commission with another broker who may have a customer. (By giving an exclusive agency to a reputable agent, you avoid the possibility of being sued for commission by one or more brokers whom you had forgotten you had listed your property with.) The owner can and should keep his agent advised of all inquiries he may get and work in harmony with him.

If you expect a broker to protect you, you should, as a matter of fairness and reciprocity, be willing to protect him by making him your exclusive agent. List your property with one live, wide-awake firm (which will only consent to push it if placed with them exclusively). It will serve you better than ten dead ones who list everything offered but sell little!

The net result of an exclusive agency: Your agent, feeling sure in due time of fair compensation for his services, will always be looking out for your best interests; he can afford to advertise your property extensively; can afford to spend the necessary time on it; can offer it safely to any brother-broker who has a customer; will secure the best price possible for you; will save you the annoyance of dealing with Tom, Dick and Harry; will do it all for you, separating "the wheat from the chaff."

Sincerely,

1-5   HOME SELLING HINTS TO PROSPECTIVE SELLERS

Dear _____:

HOME SELLING HINTS

The first step in selling your home is the selection of a competent Realtor who should:

- Know the surrounding area.
- Have an active and progressive sales force
- Have a good reputation
- Know how to correctly appraise your home
- Use modern merchandising methods

Next, in setting a sale price on your home, certain facts must not be ignored. For example, what you paid for a piece of property does not determine its current market value. Neighborhood changes, the age of the property, the usage it has had are all factors. Also, there is a distinct difference between the additional money you put into your home for replacement of worn-out items such as the water heater, shingles, or the furnace, and the added investment for capital improvements for such items as another bedroom, a garage or a family room. Maintenance helps uphold the value, but it does not add to the market value to the same extent as capital improvements.

The sale of residential real estate to a great degree is the sale of an emotion. It is next to impossible for an owner to separate the brick, mortar and lumber from the emotional memories of the life he has lived in his own home. For this reason, an owner cannot objectively set a realistic price on his home. On the other hand, a Realtor is unbiased in his opinion, and he will give you the benefit of his years of experience. You would not go to a doctor and have him give you a prescription for medicine, and then throw the medicine away. Your Realtor's advice is like your doctor's. You may not like what you hear from either one. But in the long run if you follow the Realtor's advice, your home will be sold sooner and you probably will get a better price than if you ignore his advice.

You should look at your property with cold, calculating eyes because that is what a potential purchaser will do.

Remember, first impressions are lasting impressions. Therefore, see to it that the exterior of your home is inviting:

- The lawn should be trimmed.
- The sidewalks should be edged.
- The yard should be cleaned.
- If the season is suitable have the flower beds cultivated and flowers blooming.
- Touch up anything that needs it.
- Consider the value of a quick coat of exterior paint.

Unless the interior of the home is completely run down and in bad repair, the only thing decorating will do will be to make your home more saleable. It will not get you a better price. Be critical of your property; remember everybody else will be as they go through it. Do not hesitate to make small, inexpensive repairs, and:

- Always have your home neat and tidy. Give special attention to the kitchen and bathroom as these rooms sell more homes than anything else.
- Make sure windows are sparkling clean and walls unmarred.
- Fix leaky faucets, loose doorknobs, sticky drawers and warped cabinet doors.
- Remove all unnecessary material from attic and basement to show off their full storage and utility space.
- Keep stairways clear to avoid cluttered appearance and possible accidents.
- Keep all rooms clean, bright and neatly arranged.
- Turn on lights in dark rooms and raise shades midway.
- Have porch furniture attractively placed.
- Depending on the season, have fire in fireplace or outdoor grill ready to use.

- Create the impression of relaxed family enjoyment.
- Cooperate with the Realtor in making short notice appointments for showings.

Clients with tight schedules usually are genuinely interested in buying and are more apt to make an offer than someone who can time his visit to your convenience. When the client and Realtor arrive:

- Greet them courteously—then disappear.
- Avoid having too many people present, otherwise the buyer will feel he is intruding.
- Keep children and pets out of the way.
- Turn off the radio and TV so the Realtor can talk to the buyer without distractions.
- If possible, leave the house. If this is not practical, do not tag along. Your presence will hamper free discussions. The Realtor needs to get the buyer to talk freely so he can ferret out his likes and dislikes. Knowing them, the Realtor can then "sell" the appeal of your home to his client.
- Do not volunteer any comments unless urged to do so by the Realtor.
- Do not try to interest the buyer in the purchase of rugs, furniture, etc., prior to the signing of the sales contract. This can ruin a transaction. After the sale has been made there will be plenty of time for such discussions.
- Do not discuss terms of sale, occupancy, etc. with the buyer. Refer these questions to the Realtor as the right answers may make or lose the sale.
- Subsequent to the showing, occasionally the buyer may telephone you for information or for a commitment that could be detrimental to your best interests. Again, refer him to the Realtor.

- Never let anyone into your home unless they have an appointment. If a perfect stranger rang your door bell and asked to come in, you would not ordinarily allow him in. A sign in your front yard does not change this situation. See to it that anyone asking to look at your home has the proper identification either from the listing office or of a cooperating Realtor.

Now you have only to wait for the most welcome sign of all . . .

THEY DID IT AGAIN!

Sincerely,

1-6 "WE CAN AND WE CAN'T" LETTER TO PROSPECTIVE SELLERS

Dear _____ :

WE'VE GOT A PROBLEM..............WE CAN AND
                    WE CAN'T

WE CAN'T . . .

Handle all the prospects who have been coming into our office since our Grand Opening in January. Why? Because our inventory isn't large enough to satisfy all the inquiries for residential property, commercial, acreage or condominiums.

WE DEFINITELY CAN . . .

SELL your property, when you consider selling.
GIVE you a fair opinion of market value, at no obligation.
INVITE you and your friends to drop by and see us. We'd like to show you first hand why _____ Associates, Realtors, has been successful in _____, with 9 area offices.
WE MAY BE NEW TO THE _____ AREA . . .

BUT WE'RE OLD HANDS AT THE REAL ESTATE BUSI-
                    NESS IN _____.

Let us prove it to you!

                                        Sincerely,

1-7 LETTER TO LANDOWNER COUNSELLING HIM AND SECURING A LISTING

Dear _____:

WE WOULD LIKE TO LIST YOUR PROPERTY AT:
SECTION 11, NE QUADRANT,
_____ COUNTY, _____,
FLORIDA.

It has come to our attention that you own property that, we are confident, could be profitably sold to a qualified buyer.

Our Commercial/Investment Division is actively seeking out listings of this type, since we are constantly being contacted for acreage (development property, business sites, etc.) such as yours. While our present service area concentration is in Central Florida, we are also listing properties on the West Coast.

An opinion of value of your property, as well as other information about real estate activity in the vicinity of your property, is offered to you without obligation or charge.

We have the professional know-how, the prospects, and the desire necessary to sell your property. Will you seriously consider listing it with us? Please contact us at _____.

Sincerely,

1-8 INFORMING POSSIBLE SELLERS ABOUT TRADING OPPORTUNITIES

Dear _____ :

Time to TRADE UP!!!!

Is your home too small? Are you being transferred? Need convenience? Prefer country living? Whatever your reasons for desiring a change, let me help you solve YOUR problem.

I am a Realtor Associate at _____ Realtors, and I would like to make your dream come true. My firm has many years experience and has grown progressively with your area, and therefore can offer you a TRADE plan that will work.

Enclosed   is   our   TRADE-IN   brochure   called "_____", and a copy of our Special Selling Plan to further acquaint you with our firm.

May I please visit with you to explain in detail, WITH-OUT OBLIGATION, our complete program? Call me today to arrange an appointment at your convenience.

HAPPY TRADING!!!!

Sincerely yours,

1-9 MODEL LETTER TO SECURE LISTINGS IN NICER AREAS

Dear _____:

I am writing several homeowners in your neighborhood hoping for information and assistance. By giving personalized, courteous, prompt attention, I specialize in selling homes in the nicer areas.

At present, I have sincere buyers desiring a home in your neighborhood. Therefore, if you know of anyone who is thinking of selling, I certainly would appreciate a call. Of course, there is *never* any obligation.

I would like to point out that our office stands ready 24 hours a day to serve anyone's real estate needs—whether it be buying, selling, leasing or trading. Please call or stop by our new office.

Thank you,

1-10 MODEL LETTER TO SECURE A LISTING IN FAMILIAR AREA

Dear _____:

Thank you for listening to my story. I am looking forward to meeting you. I will do a comparable analysis on your home which includes giving you an estimation of what you should net from the sale of the home in _____. There is no obligation to you. We are active in _____. In fact, two of our sales people live there, are sold on the area, and know the market very well.

Enclosed is some literature on our company. Feel free to call me anytime.

Sincerely,

1-11 PRAISE FOR A FELLOW REALTOR WHO HAS LISTED A HOME YOU WANTED TO LIST—ESTATE PROPERTY

Dear _____:

Thank you for your letter of October 4, 19___. I talked to your attorney and she stated that another Realtor in our city appraised your estate. The Realtor is an excellent one.

Your attorney said there was a pending sale to one of the heirs of the estate. My partner and I drove by the properties and we feel that this cash offer is a good one.

If we can be of further assistance, please call.

Sincerely,

1-12   MODEL LETTER TO PROSPECTIVE SELLERS ADVISING THEM TO CALL ANOTHER FIRM

Dear _____:

I want to thank you very much for calling me in regard to selling your home. As you stated in our conversation, I have a prospective purchaser for your neighbor's home. The loan on this home has not been approved and the task of attempting to sell it has been extremely difficult.

Our firm is not geared to selling properties in your area, and I will be the first to admit this. I listed your neighbor's home because he was a close friend who has purchased another home from me. I would rather be honest with you now than have you mad at me 90 days from now because we have not sold your property.

I am enclosing on a separate piece of paper the name of another Realtor who will be able to assist you in the sale of your home.

Thank you again for calling me and I wish you success in selling your home.

Sincerely,

1-13 ANOTHER REALTOR IS FOR YOU

Dear _____:

Sorry I am so late in answering your letter. I had hoped to be able to write to you sooner.

I was planning to try and drive by your lot, but I haven't found the time. Because of this, it seems I am not the right agent to list your lot—it is too far away.

My firm doesn't work with builders nor specialize in selling lots. Also, I'm unfamiliar with the values of lots in your area and I feel I would do you an injustice by trying to sell it. I am sure you understand.

I talked to several Realtors in _____ and they seem to be as unfamiliar with the area as I am. I would suggest you write to someone in the real estate business in _____ or to the person who sold you the lot.

Thank you for thinking of me. Sorry I can't help you more.

Sincerely,

Chapter 2

Tested Letters That Get You
Profitable Real Estate Listings

Here are 16 tested and effective letters that can bring you more real estate listings . . .

2-1 MODEL LETTER FOR FOLLOWING UP ON AN FSBO NEWSPAPER AD

Dear _____:

      I saw your ad in last Saturday's paper. I would appreciate it if you would take five minutes of your time and read the advantages of authorizing a Realtor to sell your home.

WHY YOU SHOULD LIST WITH A REALTOR

1. Surveys show that homes sold by brokers net more to the owner than do homes sold by the owner.
2. An average homeowner does not know the true market value. A Realtor has a modern approach to determining market value. Only a professional with knowledge of the market and market trends can offer you this service.
3. A Realtor has strength in the market place—We are in direct contact with loan companies every day, and have knowledge of the best possible financing to benefit both the buyer *and* seller. There are at least 40 ways to finance a home. Do you know how to utilize the one that will benefit you the most?
4. Are you familiar with these terms: discount points, building code inspections, title insurance, abstract extension, MGIC financing, documentary stamps? This transaction could be a little more complicated than you are anticipating.
5. Can you answer objections a prospective buyer might have about your home? Chances are they will not even arise. It's hard for a stranger to ask personal questions of a homeowner. A Realtor overcomes objections—after learning them—and this often results in a sale.
6. Can you qualify your buyer? Can you ask personal questions of him? What is his income? Is he involved in any judgments? Has there been a divorce involving child support which would complicate the purchase of a new home? Does he have outstanding debts? These are personal matters that are often not talked about freely.

7. What do you plan on spending for advertising? On the average, only 1 call out of 120 turns into a sale on the advertised property. When a home is listed with a Multiple Listing firm, it is advertised many times daily—every time a salesman shows his book to a prospective buyer. We advertise to find qualified buyers.
8. Are you really saving by selling your home on your own?

      If you have any questions, feel free to give me a call anytime. If I can be of any service, I'd be glad to talk to you.

Sincerely,

2-2 LETTER STRESSING THE DIFFICULTIES OF SELLING

Dear _____:

We understand that you are thinking of selling your home. Perhaps you feel that you can accomplish this by yourself . . . and perhaps you can. Usually, however, selling your own home results in difficulties—it's often more trouble than it's worth.

For example the potential home buyer today will ask, "What's the appraisal on your house?" They will take the appraisal figure or even less and deduct the commission to arrive at an offer. The buyer does not feel that he should pay the seller the commission. Naturally he is looking out for himself.

So in the long run, you as a seller will not be saving. In fact, you will be losing money while having many frustrations and annoyances. It is a statistical fact that homeowners who authorize a Realtor to sell their home obtain more money and relieve themselves of many problems and headaches.

Of course, you will get calls. But many will be from folks who are merely curious. Some won't even give you their names; others may use a fictitious name. People will promise to come over and then fail to show up. A few will drive by, slow up, look around, and then drive on.

Those who do inspect your property may proposition you. Will you take back a second mortgage? Will you RENT with an option to buy? And so on.

All these frustrating, time-consuming annoyances can be avoided by listing with an experienced broker. We appraise and advertise your house promptly, professionally, and without charge. We refer to our waiting list of home-seekers and select ONLY those who are (1) qualified to buy, and (2) seeking your type of house. WE show the house (you need not be present) when it is convenient for you to let us do so. We assist the buyers with financing problems; you get all cash.

All these services cost you nothing until and unless we find a BUYER! Since you have nothing to lose, why not give us a call? Our office has a lot to offer in the way of service. We can give you superior and professional real estate service. We offer a Positive Approach.

We are a small office and, being small, we are able to thoroughly concentrate our efforts on your house. A small office with knowledge, experience, and "Personal Service in Person" as its main goal is unquestionably your best choice in selling your house. You are under no obligation, but before you authorize any firm to sell your property, please allow us to visit with you.

Sincerely,

2-3 OFFERING YOUR SERVICES FOR THE FUTURE

Dear _____:

Our business is selling homes, and in watching for properties for sale, we noticed your "For Sale" sign. We realize if you had been interested in the services of a Realtor, you would have listed your property for sale with one of our local offices.

However, over the years, we have found that many homeowners eventually do list their homes for sale with Realtors. Should you decide in the future to list your home, here are some reasons why you should list with us:

1. We will prepare a generous advertising program.
2. We accept trade-in homes.
3. We arrange for financing of homes.
4. We've been selling homes since 1924.
5. We have out-of-town (as well as local) buyers.
6. We belong to a nationwide Real Estate Referral Service.
7. We have several brokers and sales associates working for you.
8. We have a home appraisal service.
9. We're professionals—and we take our profession very seriously.
10. We're serious! We do have buyers, and we need more homes to show them.

Please let us know if we can be of help in selling your home. May we hear from you?

Sincerely,

2-4   LETTER ATTEMPTING TO ARRANGE A MEETING

Dear _____:

We note that you are offering your home for sale. I assume that you are doing so because you feel that you can sell it yourself without paying a commission. But—will you actually save that commission, or will you eventually cut your price and have to handle all the technical worries that we can take care of for you?

By this time your family has been exposed to many strangers inspecting your home. You have spent money on advertising your property and time in showing it to inquisitive "lookers." You have not known whether the buyer with "X" dollars for a down payment can go through with an actual transaction.

We can relieve you of all these burdens. Our office has contacts in the fields of mortgage and title insurance that may enable us to reduce the down payment necessary for a prospective purchaser to buy your home. To this we add our experience in writing advertising, expert full-time sales people, and operating policies that protect your privacy by allowing only qualified prospects to enter and inspect your home.

I would appreciate an opportunity to meet you and answer any questions you may have. Please feel free to call on me for any help you may need.

Sincerely,

P.S. Our services cost nothing unless a sale is made.

2-5   HELPFUL HINTS FOR THE OWNER SELLING HIS OWN HOME

Dear _____:

HOMEOWNERS SELLING TIPS

THEY SEE THE OUTSIDE FIRST!

You'll want your home to say "I'm CHARMING, I'm WARM, I'm HOME."

—Paint those downspouts and gutters and the front door. (It's through this entrance all your prospects will pass.)

—Keep your yard, gardens and driveways neat and clean. Keep toys in the back yard.

—Buyers always overestimate the costs of painting and redecorating. Invariably these overestimated costs are subtracted from your asking price before an offer to purchase is made. Often $200 spent in redecorating will return $500 to $1000 in additional selling price.

—Be a Mr. Fixit or call in your plumber and carpenter. Leaky faucets and warped or sticky doors mean lower offers from your prospects.

—Clean up and clean out from basement to attic. The extra effort will repay you many times over. Attics free of clutter make your home look roomier, cleaner.

—Lights on all over the house. Warmth and coziness sell. Buyers want to see your home—if they can't "see" they won't buy.

If you are trying to sell your home, you will be expected to furnish certain vital information on your property such as:

1. Asking price—Room sizes—Lot size and dimensions.
2. Mortgage information—Balances to date on 1st & 2nd Trusts—Monthly payments.
3. A plat or survey.
4. Zoning data current and proposed.
5. Real estate taxes.

6. Mortgage loan commitment—FHA and/or VA appraisal.
7. Amount of cash necessary to purchase—Loan placement fees.
8. Total settlement costs for buyer—Deposit needed.
9. Monthly utility bills.
10. Schools, churches, stores, bus.
11. Accurate comparable sales of homes in your neighborhood.
12. A contract of sale.

BE CAREFUL WHAT YOU SAY!

—Most home owners love their home so much that they fail to take an objective point of view when pointing out its selling points. Don't oversell. Above all, do not withhold information on its defects—especially hidden ones.

—Children and pets are cute and lovable but are best kept away from while you are showing or negotiating.

—TV and radio usually add to the confusion. Hi-Fi or stereo are all right if kept soft and low. (However, no vocals or rock and roll, please.)

We hope that the above may prove helpful. Being helpful is part of the service we furnish. If we can be of further service, won't you pick up the phone and dial _____.

Please ask for _____

_____ & Co., Inc.

2-6 EMPHASIZING A "UNIQUE MARKETING PLAN"

Dear _____:

I noticed your home for sale. It appears to be a very nice home, and I am sure it is. Many people, like yourself, would love to own it.

By now you may realize that selling your own home is time-consuming, frustrating and complicated! You might have even reached the point where you are considering asking help from a Realtor, but you don't have anyone special in mind.

Our company knows your area and we have a Unique Marketing Plan that we would like to discuss with you. Because we like your home and your area, we would welcome the opportunity to be your Realtor.

I am fortunate to have been selected to work the area in which your home is located. I live in the area and have had excellent success in this location. In fact, I have personally sold over 20 homes in this fine area.

I am not going to pester you, but if you should desire the services of a Realtor who knows your area and has had excellent success in it, please call me.

Sincerely,

2-7 MODEL LETTER TELLING OF YOUR SERVICES

Dear _____:

     Thank you for visiting with me concerning the selling of your home.

     FOR PROSPECTIVE SELLERS, WE OFFER:

1. Honesty & integrity above all else. Check with any banker, broker or attorney in the _____ district.
2. Over 100 salesmen and brokers working on your behalf.
3. Several conveniently located offices to meet at and work from.
4. Our buyer memory bank data processed _____ machine with its lighted display panel insures none of our buyers are overlooked.
5. Courteous showings at convenient hours by our helpful associates.
6. A terrific sales record—1st in sales for many years in the _____ district.
7. Free referral service and aid in moving out of town.
8. Advice on what to do, and WHAT NOT TO DO, to aid in selling your property at the highest obtainable market value.
9. Services of 3 M.L.S. Boards of Realtors.
10. Financing arranged for our buyers at numerous places.
11. Financially qualified buyers, to prevent numerous needless showings.
12. Signs and Open Houses when helpful but only used with seller's permission.
13. Trade-ins taken and arranged.
14. Strict adherence to the Realtor's Code of Ethics.

     I will contact you Monday concerning your home.

                    Sincerely,

2-8 LETTER STRESSING SEVEN QUALIFICATIONS

Dear _____:

Perhaps you have made a decision to sell your property!! Please allow ME to explain how YOU will benefit by having me represent you. Certainly you'd like the most money you can get, as quickly as you can get it, with as few problems as possible. Isn't that right?

Here are just a few of our services and qualifications:

1. _____ Realty, Inc. has been a successful and leading real estate firm since August, 1955. Check our reputation for honesty and results with any attorney, or banker in the _____ district.
2. Mr. _____, C.R.B. is the first "Certified Residential Broker" in the _____ and _____ counties.
3. _____ Realty, Inc. can present your home to qual- ified buyers through our staff of nearly 100 salesmen and brokers.
4. Our _____ Buyer Finding Computer eliminates human errors in matching buyers to property.
5. We can help you determine the right price. You may need a professional "Opinion of Value."
6. We arrange financing and cut through a lot of red tape.
7. Our firm is one of the very, very few firms that are members of three Multiple Listing Boards of Realtors—_____, _____ and _____.

This is only the beginning of our success story for you. Take advantage of our free advice and opinions, in the privacy of your home.

Competent professional service, action and satisfaction. You deserve it!! At your convenience, allow us to help you. You'll be glad you did.

Sincerely,

2-9 "SPREADING THE WORD" ABOUT YOUR SERVICES

Dear _____:

      I would like to spread the word that I am at your service and would welcome the opportunity of visiting with you regarding your present or future real estate needs.

      As you may have heard, our office enjoys the reputation of many years of experience in appraisal and sales of residential properties, and sales and management of investment properties. Both our clients and our customers have benefited from our counsel. We consider every property important to us regardless of size.

      As professionals, we can offer many immediate as well as long term advantages to our client sellers. The correct market value of your property is determined; curiosity seekers are eliminated; approximately 44 cooperating licensed Realtors are advised of the availability; showings are made by appointment only and at your convenience. Pictures of your property with pertinent information are displayed in our office and distributed to more than 250 sales associates.

      If you are not in the market to sell at this time, help me "spread the word" to your friends and relatives who are. For that purpose I am enclosing several business cards. Please tell your friends & relatives to ask for me when calling the office.

      Thank you.

                       Sincerely,

      We are open 72 hours per week to serve you

2-10   MODEL LETTER TO PAST CLIENTS AND FRIENDS

Dear _____ :

Just a note to say "Hello!" Please keep this card as a ready reference. If I can ever be of service to you or your friends in real estate needs, feel free to call me anytime. I would certainly appreciate hearing from you or your friends. Our firm is a member of the _____ Real Estate Board and the *all important* Multiple Listing Service. We also offer a full line of insurance and rental management. We are also associated with a fine builder of custom homes. *We are looking for listings.* Please keep us in mind among your friends and acquaintances.

Thank you,

2-11   A THANK YOU FOR ALLOWING A HOME INSPECTION

Dear _____ :

Thank you for your courtesy in extending to our salesmen the privilege of inspecting your fine home.

It will be a sincere pleasure to show our home prospects your caliber of home, and you may be assured that we will do our best to negotiate a satisfactory sale of your property.

Sincerely yours,

2-12   THANK YOU FOR VISITING WITH OUR SALES ASSOCIATE

Dear _____:

    I want to thank you for giving Ms. _____ of our company the opportunity to visit with you and to discuss the selling of your home.

    Ms. _____ is a capable associate, and I know she can be of immeasurable help to you.

    If in any way I personally can be of assistance, please do not hesitate to call me.

Sincerely,

2-13   LETTER TELLING OF A POSSIBLE BUYER

Dear _____:

    I have an investor who might be interested in purchasing your property. The client I am working with would purchase your property subject to it being rezoned. He would pay the current market value of the property less the cost of rezoning.

    I will contact you this weekend to discuss this matter.

Sincerely,

2-14   INFORMING AN OWNER THAT A CASH BUYER IS INTERESTED

Dear _____:

     I want to thank you for visiting with me concerning your nice home. It is located in a fine area.

     As I mentioned to you, I have a cash buyer who might be a good prospect. My prospect wants a ranch type home close to transportation and work. Your home fits all three of these needs.

     If you should decide to sell your home in the near future, please call me and we will make arrangements to inspect your property.

                                 Sincerely,

2-15   LETTER THANKING A REFERRAL FOR VISITING

Dear _____:

     Thank you for visiting with me about the possibility of our firm being authorized to sell your home.

     As I mentioned to you in our conversation, _____, our mutual friend, asked me to call you. He purchased a home from me seven years ago and was happy with the professional service rendered to him and his family.

     When I can be of assistance to you in selling your home, please call me.

                                 Sincerely,

2-16   MODEL LETTER OFFERING AN APPRAISAL

Dear _____:

I had lunch with Konnie _____ yesterday and he mentioned you were planning to build a home in South Carolina.

I am assuming that you will be wanting to sell your home here in _____. I would like to inspect the home for you and give you an appraisal of what it may sell for.

Our office is probably one of the most active in residential sales in _____ County.

Should you decide to sell, I would certainly appreciate the opportunity to handle the sale for you.

Sincerely yours,

Chapter 3

Following Up After the Listing Has Been Secured With Effective Model Letters

The following 11 letters will help you reassure your listings of your active interest in selling their property . . .

3-1   THANK YOU LETTER FROM THE BROKER

Dear _____:

Thank you for your confidence in letting us represent you in the sale of your property. We assure you that every effort will be made to obtain the best price and conditions most favorable to you in today's market. If at any time matters arise that you would like to discuss, please do not hesitate to call.

We are proud of our sales record, and with your cooperation, I am sure we will be successful in the sale of your property. Mr. _____, who listed your property for sale, is highly regarded in the real estate field and will keep you informed.

Your good will is our greatest asset and we are pledged to your service. We are looking forward to a pleasant and fruitful business relationship.

Very truly yours,

3-2 LETTER THANKING AND INSTRUCTING THE SELLER

Dear _____:

Thank you for listing your real estate with _____, Realtors. Our goal is to sell your home in the shortest possible time, for the highest possible price, with the least amount of inconvenience to you.

Enclosed is a copy of your listing we sent to the Multiple Listing Service. Please examine it for any possible errors or omissions. If any corrections should be made contact our office immediately so we can make them. Our salesmen will be using the information on this sheet when talking with their prospective clients and we don't want your home to be misrepresented.

We welcome the opportunity to be of service to you. If a prospect should come to your door as a result of the sign, advertising, referral or word of mouth, it is advisable to give out very little information and not allow them to enter your home. Instead, request their name and phone number and refer them to us. We will follow up immediately, first to qualify them and then to arrange a convenient time for a showing.

Since we cooperate with all Realtors and are more than happy to give them all the necessary facts they need to help us sell your home, none should approach you. If they do, get the salesman's name and his company's name and we will contact them.

If you have any questions at this time, please feel welcome to call us. Our desire is to serve you well.

Sincerely,

3-3   THANKING THE SELLER AND OFFERING A RELOCATION SERVICE

Dear _____:

We are pleased to have this opportunity to act as your Exclusive Realtor and thank you for listing your home with us.

Our well-trained sales staff will make a sincere and determined effort to sell your home. We will qualify our clients prior to calling you for an appointment. We believe that we can relieve you of the many responsibilities and details of the sale.

It is understood that we have your consent to advertise your property at our discretion.

We are members of _____ Service which is a professional real estate service designed for families on the move. There is no cost (or obligation) to you. Let us bring you together with a Realtor in your new location who can help find you a new home and make this move a lot more enjoyable. Please call _____ our Nationwide Coordinator _____ _____ if you want this service, and we will do the rest.

We assure you of our desire to be of "Real Service."

Sincerely,

3-4 REASSURING THE SELLER OF YOUR EXPERT SERVICES

Dear _____:

We wish to express to you, as a client, our thanks for the confidence you have shown in our organization. Your partronage and good will constitute a real asset, and we trust our collective efforts in serving you will warrant continued confidence in us.

By listing your property with us, you recruited the expert service and knowledge of trained personnel whose one objective is to do a good job for you. We appreciate your calling on us and want to assure you that our well-trained office and sales staff will endeavor to do everything possible to conclude a prompt and satisfactory sale for you.

Your cooperation in maintaining and showing your property will be a help in obtaining a qualified buyer in the shortest possible time—this is a cooperative project. I am enclosing a "Property Showing" brochure which provides some guidelines.

Please feel free to stop by or call anytime. We are always ready to serve your real estate needs.

Sincerely,

3-5   MODEL LETTER WELCOMING COMMENTS FROM THE SELLER

Dear _____:

      We are pleased that you have selected us to represent you as your agent in the sale of your property. Speaking on behalf of the _____ Company, we congratulate you on your choice and would like to thank you for the confidence which you have placed in us.

      I am enclosing some data and policies on our firm, which I hope you will read over and then attach to your listing card.

      The sales counselor who listed your property is always available for consultation and will be contacting you regularly, reporting to you on the progress being made toward a SALE! Should the sales counselor be unable to answer your questions, please contact me personally and I will be happy to discuss them with you.

      We also want to stress that if you are unhappy with us in any way, please let me know, since this is the only way we have of correcting what we are doing wrong.

      Remember, the only way we receive a fee is if your home sells, so let's work together towards our common goal, THE SALE.

              Yours For Happy Selling,

3-6 TELLING THE SELLER HOW HE CAN HELP SELL HIS PROPERTY

Dear _____:

Thank you for giving us the opportunity to sell your home. We will do our best to sell it as soon as possible. You can help in several ways. Just as you like to patronize stores that have a bright and cheerful appearance, so buyers are influenced by the appearance of your home. Here are a few tips that we find helpful.

• Most prospects wish to see the closets; make sure that yours are neat. A cluttered appearance makes them look smaller than they actually are.

• Get little things repaired. Loose door knobs, hangers, crooked light fixtures are all small things in themselves, and you probably don't notice them because you are used to them, but they make a bad impression on prospects.

• Keep the yard and grounds as attractive as possible. Flowers and flower boxes add to the appearance of most homes.

• Let the salesperson show the home without your assistance. He can call you if he needs some information, but real estate is his business and he knows the prospect. Many prospects are afraid to ask questions if the owner is around.

We will always phone in advance before bringing any prospect to see your home. However, we would appreciate your leaving a key with us since many people only have time to look for a home on the weekends. In this way, you will be free to come and go and enjoy your weekends too.

Sincerely,

3-7   MODEL LETTER EXPLAINING RULES FOR HOME SHOWINGS

Dear _____:

THANK YOU, as we add your home to our listings. We would like to express our appreciation of this evidence of your faith in the name of _____ Company, a name we want to stand for excellence in sales, service and satisfaction. In doing business, it will always be our aim to continue to deserve your patronage.

SHOWMANSHIP HELPS SALESMANSHIP SELL HOMES

We have your home for sale because we want to sell it. With a little effort on your part, this can be accomplished quickly and at the right price. Here are 20 friendly tips to help you and us show your home to its best advantage. Some of them may be applicable to you or your home. We find our efforts are most successful when the stage is well set.

PREPARATION FOR SHOWING

1. First impressions are lasting ones. An inviting exterior insures inspection of the interior. Keep the lawn trimmed; the flower beds cultivated; the yard free and clear of refuse.
2. Decorate your home—a step toward a SALE. Faded walls and worn woodwork reduce the desire to buy. Don't tell a prospect how it *will* look—show him by redecorating first. A quicker sale at a higher price will be the result.
3. Cleanliness is next to Godliness. Bright, cheery windows and unmarred walls will assist your sale.
4. Fix that faucet! Dripping water discolors and calls attention to faulty plumbing.
5. Spend a day with the carpenter! Loose door knobs, sticking drawers, warped cabinet doors, etc., are noticed by the prospect. Have them fixed!
6. From top to bottom—remove all unnecessary articles that have accumulated. Display the full value of your storage and utility space from basement to attic.

7. Step High, Step Low! Your prospect will do just that unless all passageways are cleared of objects. Avoid cluttered appearances and possible injuries.

8. Closet illusions. Clothes properly hung, shoes, hats and other articles neatly placed, will make your closet appear more adequate.

9. DEAR TO THE HEART is the kitchen. Colorful curtains in harmony with the floor and counter tops add appeal.

10. Check and double check your bath. Bright and clean bathrooms sell many homes.

11. For the rest of your life. Bedrooms are outstanding features, arrange them neatly.

12. Can you see the light? Illumination is a WELCOME SIGN. For after-dark inspection, turn on the lights from the front through the house. A prospect will feel a "glowing warmth" otherwise impossible to attain.

SHOWING THE HOUSE

13. "Three's a Crowd," more will lose the SALE. Avoid having too many people present during the inspection. The prospect will feel like an intruder and hurry through.

14. Music is Mellow—but don't have any on during the showing of the house. Shut off the radio; it distracts. Let the salesman and buyer talk, free of such disturbances.

15. Love me, Love my dog—doesn't apply in house selling. Keep pets out of the way—preferably out of the house.

16. Silence is Golden! Be courteous but don't force conversation with the prospect. He is there to inspect your home, not to pay a social call.

17. Be It Ever So Humble! Never apologize for the appearance of the house, after all, it has been lived in. Let our salesman answer any objections when raised—this is his job.

18. In the Shadows. Please don't tag along with the prospect and salesman. He knows the buyer's requirements and can better point out the features of your home when alone. You will be called if needed.
19. Putting the Cart Before the Horse. Trying to dispose of furniture and furnishings to the prospect before the purchase of the home often loses a sale. Proper timing is important.
20. A Word to the Wise. DO NOT DISCUSS price, terms, possession or other factors with the prospect. Refer them to us. We are better equipped to bring the negotiations to a favorable conclusion with all due speed. We ask that you show your home to prospective customers only by appointment through this office. Your cooperation will be appreciated and lead to a more prompt conclusion to the sale.

Again, OUR THANKS,

3-8 "HELPFUL HINTS" FOR HOME SELLING

Dear _____:

I wish to take this opportunity to express my appreciation for the confidence you have shown in our organization by listing the above captioned property with us, and we shall do all in our power to dispose of your property as expediently as possible.

I am enclosing herewith a confirmation of your Listing Agreement, a pamphlet entitled "Helpful Hints" and other company brochures, which I trust you will find time to read.

Please feel free to contact me at any time.

Sincerely yours,

HELPFUL HINTS . . .

Now that we have placed your house for sale we ask that you read this interesting little pamphlet. We have listed herein a few helpful hints that will make the selling of your house an easier and more pleasant task for us and you the home owner.

Selling a house is not unlike selling any other commodity. People shop and buy best in well organized stores. Houses are no exception.

Check all the closets in your home and make sure that every one is in good order and not cluttered. Carefully arranged closets will appear to be much larger than they really are.

Replace all burned out light bulbs and repair all faulty light switches. Little things sometimes hinder a sale more than a large repair.

HELPFUL HINTS . . .

Badly cracked plaster, loose door knobs, crooked light fixtures are among the small items that are easily repaired and cause the most embarrassment and give a bad impression.

Be sure to arrange shades or drapes to get a maximum amount of light in dark rooms. Light colors will add cheerfulness in dark kitchens and pantries.

Be sure to supply us with accurate figures on taxes, fuel bills and tell us of any major improvement lately done such as a new roof, etc.

When one of our sales representatives is showing your house to a prospect, never volunteer any information unless asked and then supply only the essential facts.

HELPFUL HINTS . . .

Buyers ask a great many questions of our representatives when being shown through a house and want to do this out of hearing of the home owner. They feel more at ease, so it is much better that the inspection proceed without your immediate presence.

Remember that if an offer is made that is acceptable it is better to accept it on the spot. It may never be repeated.

In closing please be reminded that all of our staff and our years of experience are at your disposal and we will be glad to give you expert advice on any problems or questions that may arise.

3-9 INTRODUCING THE SALESMAN AND THE MLS PROGRAM

Dear _____:

Enclosed is your signed copy of the agreement listing your property for sale with _____ & Co. in cooperation with the Multiple Listing Service Association. Please read it again carefully and if you have any questions be sure to call. We'll be glad to be of help.

Regarding the showing of your home, MLS salespeople will phone in advance for appointments whenever possible. Occasionally, however, a salesman may stop at your door unannounced, with a prospect. We want you to know that you are in no way obligated to admit a salesman without an appointment, but it will be advantageous to permit a showing to every prospect if at all possible.

We shall appreciate your advising us if you are in any way dissatisfied with the services of the Multiple Listing Service. We are anxious to maintain a high standard of performance.

The sale of real estate is an important, expensive and often complicated transaction. We, therefore, strongly advise you to retain an attorney to handle the closing of the sale and to draw the deed and other documents which, by law, we cannot draw for you. If you desire, we can provide you with a list of attorneys from which to choose. Please advise us of counsel's name when you engage him so we may work together for your best interests.

This listing will receive the immediate attention of _____, our salesman, who will be handling your account personally. He will welcome any calls from you. Please contact _____ whenever you desire to inquire about the progress to date in the sale of your property.

Thank you for this opportunity to be of service to you in the sale of this property. You may be assured that we will give our attention and effort to bring about the desired sale in a manner most pleasing to you.

Sincerely,

3-10   MODEL LETTER INCLUDING A 10 POINT QUESTIONNAIRE

Dear _____:

      It will assist us in advertising and merchandising your home if you would kindly answer the questions below. (Please list responses in order of importance.)

1. What were the five most important reasons your family has for selecting your home?

    (a) _____
    (b) _____
    (c) _____
    (d) _____
    (e) _____

2. What are the five things about your home that your family has enjoyed the most?

    (a) _____
    (b) _____
    (c) _____
    (d) _____
    (e) _____

Thank you for your cooperation.

Owner: _____

Address: _____

                               Sincerely,

3-11   LETTER TELLING OF WEEKLY CONTACT

Dear _____:

Thank you for listing your property for sale with us. We promise to do everything we can to sell it for you. Information on advertising, calls received, and people contacted will be furnished you every week by your representative.

If you have any questions, at any time, please call your representative, Ms. _____.

Sincerely,

Chapter 4

Dealing With the Seller During and After the Sale With Proven Letters

The 32 model letters in this key chapter will help you keep the lines of communication open with your listings and smooth the way for the closing . . .

4-1 MODEL LETTER SENDING LISTING AGREEMENT AND EXPLAINING SELLING PRICE

Dear _____:

Enclosed is our listing agreement. After checking with _____ Company, I feel that your home should be placed on the market at $30,950. The appraisal company placed the value at $30,500. The closer we are to market value, the better off we will be.

We can proceed immediately with selling your home as soon as we receive the contract back. Please retain the second copy and return the other two.

I will date the contract when it returns. It will be a 90-day listing.

Thank you.

Sincerely,

4-2   FOLLOWING UP AFTER A PHONE CONVERSATION WITH A LISTING AGREEMENT

Dear _____:

Enclosed is the listing contract your wife discussed with you over the telephone. Kindly sign the two copies, above your wife's signature and return them to me in the enclosed self-addressed envelope.

I am very optimistic at this time about selling your home, and feel that the type of advertising I intend to use will bring a sale soon.

You have a very lovely home and I am very enthused about it. I appreciate being given the opportunity to sell it for you. I will appreciate your returning the enclosed forms as soon as possible.

Thank you, and we will proceed immediately.

Sincerely,

4-3 LETTER INFORMING SELLER THAT A BUYER'S LOAN WAS NOT APPROVED

Dear _____:

I am sorry to inform you that Mr. & Mrs. _____ were turned down for their loan.

I am enclosing a new listing agreement and a check for $250.00 (one month's rent). The _____ will be moving from your house approximately October 15. If they stay beyond the 15th, they will pay a pro rata day rent. They have taken good care of the property.

We will immediately begin pushing for a sale. Please return the 1st and 3rd copies of the listing agreement as soon as possible. We cannot advertise the house until we have the listing contract.

As you recall, the F.H.A. appraisal was $30,250. This is the price at which the property should be listed.

Thank you, and we will work very hard to obtain a satisfactory sale for you.

Sincerely,

4-4 COVER LETTER FOR MLS "HOME PHOTO GUIDE"

Dear _____:

Enclosed you will find your home featured in the newest service available—The Multiple Listing Service *Home Photo Guide*. It will be distributed to 110,000 people and represents just one of the many means we are using to market your home.

Sincerely,

4-5 LETTER PASSING ALONG PROSPECTS' REACTION TO A SHOWING

Dear _____:

I thought you might be interested to hear that we have had four more inquiries since my last offer was sent to you.

On August 19th I thought I had the house sold. The husband felt it was the nicest home he had seen for the money, *but* the wife didn't want it because of all the paneling. I suggested several ways of redoing the home to get her interested, but to no avail. The other inquiries did not call back.

Our listing is up September 3rd, and of course we would be most happy to renew our listing with you again. The forms are enclosed for your signature.

I want you to know that we have done everything possible to sell your home. We have never turned down an opportunity to show it. I would like to list some of the comments I have heard from people who have gone through the house:

1. Price is too high
2. House is too old
3. Oil heat and well
4. Too much paneling
5. Too much repair work needs to be done
6. Gravel driveway
7. No air conditioning

On the positive side:

1. Beautiful lot and trees
2. Excellent room arrangement
3. Plentiful living area
4. Beautiful bathroom
5. Privacy
6. Close to schools

The house has been shown approximately nineteen times and there have been many phone calls. I think the high interest rate, which in turn makes higher payments, and the discount points you would have to pay (7½), is what is keeping this house from selling. I am not trying to make excuses for not selling your home, because I believe that no one could have done more than we have.

I would appreciate hearing from you.

Very sincerely yours,

4-6   LETTER WARNING THAT FORECLOSURE IS IMMINENT

Dear _____:

I assume that you have been notified, as we have, that Commercial Savings & Loan has started foreclosure proceedings on your property here in _____. Bearing this in mind, I am requesting that you consider lowering the price so that we may change our advertising and possibly get a quicker sale.

We had another open house last Sunday; four couples came through the house. Counting the Open Houses and personal salesman showings, your house has been shown approximately 12 times.

There have been two derogatory comments that we feel indicate what has been holding up getting an offer. Of course, the first is the matter of taxes, but we feel we have justified this in our sales approach.

The second is that the quality of the home does not justify the $35,950 price. We are therefore suggesting that you reduce the price to $32,950. This is your decision. We are trying our best, and will continue to do our best to sell your house at the listed price or at the new suggested reduced price.

I am enclosing the necessary forms for you to sign. If you decide to lower the price as we suggested, it will require both of your signatures. Kindly fill in the price where we have indicated. Please keep the third copy for your files.

Yours truly,

4-7   KEEPING THE SELLER UP-TO-DATE

Dear _____:

I am still working very hard to sell your property. As I mentioned in the beginning, this type of property does take time to sell.

As you advised, I am sending you the names of the top four prospects who still have an interest and to whom I have devoted much time.

These four are as follows:

Mr. and Mrs. _____

Mr. and Mrs. _____

Mr. and Mrs. _____

Mr. and Mrs. _____

I will do all I can to sell one of these parties.

I still feel that it would be a wiser decision on your part to allow my firm to continue with a listing contract, because of the wide exposure that we can give. Our staff is growing. Also we can show your property in our exclusive magazine that goes to approximately 2,000 friends, clients and other business people in the community, every two months.

I will call you next week and keep you posted of my progress. Please reconsider my suggestion to retain your properties on the open market.

Thank you again for your past confidence in our firm.

Your friend,

4-8 CHECKING ON GUARANTEES

Dear _____:

Please allow me to introduce myself. I represent Mr. & Mrs. _____ in the sale of your property at _____ South 93rd Street.

Mr. _____ mentioned to me that he had talked with you over the telephone. In your conversation the topics of the roof and the air conditioner compressor arose. Mr. _____ stated that you had said the roof was a lifetime one and that the air conditioner was only three years old. He asked me to check and see if there were any guarantees on these items, and if so, would they be assignable.

I asked the closing salesman to ask you about the guarantees. You mentioned in your return letter that all of the guarantees were in a kitchen drawer. Many guarantees were there, but not any for the roof or the air conditioner.

If you have any idea of where they might be, please notify me. If not, can you remember who put on the roof and who installed the air conditioner?

If you can shed any additional light on the subject, we would appreciate it. Thank you.

Sincerely,

4-9 MODEL LETTER EXPLAINING A NEW "COMPETITIVE MARKET ANALYSIS"

Dear _____:

    I want to bring you up-to-date on the progress of the sale of your home at _____ Country Club Boulevard.

    The traffic through your house has been more than adequate to sell it. The buying public has made the following comments:

1. The house needs too much work for this price—kitchen floor repair, complete redecorating, ceiling repair possibly needed in living room and near ½ bath on 1st floor.
2. The house listed at _____ No. 56th St. is a four bedroom and in much better condition. This home sold on August 25, for $32,500. In addition to the four bedrooms, it has central air conditioning. (This is the home you asked me to check out.)

    I am not criticizing your house, but only telling you what the buying public is saying. This is my responsibility to you.

    I have some suggestions to make:

1. I think your house should be reduced to 30,950. I feel at this time the selling bracket will be around 30,000. (See attached, new comparative analysis sheet). As I told you, we always try to secure the highest possible market price. We have thoroughly exposed your property to the buying public, and the buying public is resisting the price.
2. I would also suggest that we be given an extension to October 12, 19__, because September generally is a good month for sales. We would certainly continue to push hard to sell your home.

    Enclosed you will find a form for the extension and the price reduction. If you have any questions, please call me.

Your friend,

KIRBY·YOWELL
CO.
REALTORS

9123 BEDFORD AVENUE
OMAHA, NEBRASKA 6813
PHONE 572-7770

COMPETITIVE MARKET ANALYSIS

PROPERTY ADDRESS_____Country Club Ave_____DATE_____

FOR SALE NOW.	BED RMS	BATH'S	DEN	SQ. FT	1ST LOAN	LIST PRICE	DAYS ON MARKET	TERMS
Country Club Av	3	1½	no	2000	yes	31,500	20	Cash, FHA VA Conv.
No. ____	3	3/4	no	1900	yes	30,500	27	Cash, FHA, VA, Conv.
2712 No. ____ St.	3	2	yes	2100	yes	32,950	35	Cash, FHA, VA, Conv.

SOLD PAST 12 MOS.	BED RMS	BATHS	DEN	SQ FT	1ST LOAN	LIST PRICE	DAYS ON MARKET	DATE SOLD	SALE PRICE	TERMS
Country Club Av	3	2	no	1750	no	29,950	30	7/6/	29,000	VA
2516 No. ____ St.	3	1 3/4	no	1800	no	28,950	27	6/7	27,000	Conv.

EXPIRED PAST 12 MOS.	BED RMS	BATHS	DEN	SQ FT	1ST LOAN	LIST PRICE	DAYS ON MARKET	TERMS
Country Cl. Av.	3	1½	no	2100	no	34,950	90	Cash, VA, FHA, Conv.
No. ____ St.	3	2	no	2000	no	34,500	90	Cash, Conv.
2814 ____ St.	3	1 3/4	no	2100	no	35,950	90	Cash, Conv. MGIC

MARKETING POSITION

1. FINE LOCATION_____yes_____
2. EXCITING EXTRAS_____none_____
3. EXTRA SPECIAL FINANCING_____no_____
4. EXCEPTIONAL APPEAL_____average_____

BUYER APPEAL

1. WHY ARE THEY SELLING To obtain property to raise
2. HOW SOON MUST THEY SELL____60 days____
3. WILL THEY LIST AT COMPETITIVE MARKET VALUE..YES_X_NO___

ASSETS____brick, good location, space for family dining room_____
DRAWBACKS__needs redecorating, repair, no central air_____
AREA MARKET CONDITIONS_____Good_____

RECOMMENDED TERMS____Cash, VA, FHA, MGIC, Conv._____

TOP COMPETITIVE MARKET VALUE . . . . $___30,950___

PROBABLE FINAL SALES PRICE . . . . $___30,000___

APPRAISAL FORM (WORKSHEET)

COMPARABLES		SUBJECT PROPERTY	
1. ADDRESS ___ Country Club Ave.		___ Country Club Ave.	
1759 $29,000	Sq. Ft	2025	$33,557.14
	Bed Rm.		
1.75	Baths	1.5	−200.00
	Fam. Rm		
no	Rec. Rm	100'	+217.00
2 rooms	Carp	none	−400.00
	Fireplace		
Dishwasher & disposal	Kit App.	No DW & Disp	−250.00
	A/C		
2 car	Garage	1 car	−1000.00
	Lot		
	Loc		
	Cond.		
4 rooms	Drapes	6 rooms	+200.00
			$32,124.14

TOTALS

2. ADDRESS ___ No.55th ___   ___ Country Club Ave. ___

1800	$27,000	Sq. Ft.	2025	$30,375.00
		Bed Rm		
Utility shower in basement			no shower	−50.00
		Fam Rm		
	250′	Rec Rm	100′	−343.00
		Carp/drapes		−600.00
		Fireplace		
Dishwasher & Disposal		Kit App	no	−250.00
	Central	A/C	2 window	−1000.00
		Garage		
		Lot		
		Loc		
		Cond		

$28,230.00

TOTALS   Average Comparables $30,178.07
Proposed Listing Price   30,950.00
Probable Sales Bracket   30,000.00

4-10   LETTER OBTAINING MAINTENANCE APPROVAL FROM AN ABSENTEE SELLER

Dear _____

TO ALL ABSENTEE OWNERS

Address _____ Name _____

To help your listing broker in case of emergency, would you please fill in this form.

	Name	Phone
Person checking your home	_____	_____
Heating Co. (Fuel & Repairs)	_____	_____
Plumber	_____	_____
Insurance Agent	_____	_____
Lawyer	_____	_____
Snow Removal	_____	_____
Lawn Care	_____	_____

Your broker CANNOT assume the responsibility for protection and care of an empty house. In the event of an emergency, your broker would probably be the person called, so this check sheet will be of great use. Please call your insurance agent and make sure you are fully covered for any accident that might occur in a vacant house. Please fill in your out-of-town address and phone number for our records.

_____
Owner

_____   _____
New Address (Street & City)   New Phone No.

Cordially,

4-11 SUGGESTING PRICE ADJUSTMENTS

Dear _____:

I want to bring you up-to-date concerning the activity on your property located at _____ North 69th. I have tried to call you before, but I must have called at bad times.

We have had an average amount of activity on your home, but we have had no other offers since the first, which was unsatisfactory.

I have the following suggestions, Mr. & Mrs. _____
_____:

1. Adjust the price to $32,500. As I mentioned to you at the beginning of the listing, we want to obtain for our clients the highest possible price. I sincerely feel that we have given maximum effort at $34,500 to no avail. We have two new sales associates, one whom you know quite well, _____
_____. I was hoping that these two would have prospects, but again the price has been the stumbling block.

I am enclosing a market analysis sheet for you to examine. I feel that we will get much more activity at $32,500. I think the final price will be in the $32,000 range. We will push for the highest possible amount.

2. I would like an extension until October 17, 19__. September is a good month for sales. We will give it everything we have.

I am enclosing a form for adjusting the price to $32,500 and extending the listing to October 17, 19__.

Your friend,

4-12   THE 30-60 DAY REPORT FORM

Dear _____:

　　　　Enclosed you will find a report showing the activity on your property with some constructive suggestions and advice.

30-60 DAY REPORT TO OWNERS

PROPERTY	OWNER	DATE LISTED
_____Izard	Mr. and Mrs. _____	4-28-__

NAME OF PROSPECT	CONTACT	COMMENT
_____	601- _____	Not interested now

SUGGESTIONS & ADVICE

1. Allow us an extension until September 1, _____.
2. Adjust price to 30,950. Your net result will be basically the same. The closer we get to the market the better chance for the top dollar you will have. We are still very enthused about your property, and no other company will expose it more. I think lowering the price is wise and prudent at this time. If this is satisfactory to you, please sign the enclosed change-of-price form and return it to me. I will date it. If there are any questions, please call me. Thank you.

　　　　　　　　　　　　　　　　　　Sincerely,

4-13   LETTER SUGGESTING A PRICE REDUCTION AND LISTING EXTENSION

Dear _____:

I am sorry the offers we had could not have been higher, but that's what we run into many times. I have given much thought to your property and have also checked others for sale in the area.

I know that both you and your company want the honest result of this thinking and checking. There are two properties close by yours that I have checked on. The properties are _____ Browne Street and _____ North 49th Ave. These houses are basically the same home as yours. _____ Browne St. has been F.H.A. appraised at $31,800 and is on the market at $30,950. In fact, it has been on the market for two years. The home at _____ North 49th is on the market at $30,500. It was "sold," but the purchaser backed out from the sale.

I cite these examples for two reasons. The first is that appraisal and market price are not one and the same in all given areas. In this area, houses are listed below and are selling below appraisals. _____ Realtors sold a 4-bedroom Cape Cod on _____ Street which was listed at $36,500 for $32,000. Unfortunately, this area has really taken a beating as far as market price is concerned.

The second reason is that after careful consideration I feel the market value on your home is around $30,500. To be successful at all, your home should be reduced to $30,950. The closer we come to the market value the better the final figure will be. We got a low offer on your home primarily because we are out of the market at $31,950. When a home is out of the market, low offers naturally follow.

The company may say that they don't mind sitting on a house for 2 or 3 years, but believe me, this is not a prudent thing to

do. The longer a home sits the more of a white elephant it
becomes, and the final net figure is bound to be low. I feel that if
we have it listed at $30,950, it should sell somewhere around
$30,500.

I am enclosing the necessary papers for a price reduction
and an extension. Please talk to your company. At $31,950 we are
out of competition and beating our heads against a stone wall . . .

Sincerely,

4-14 THANK YOU FOR EXTENDING A LISTING

Dear _____:

Just the shortest of notes to again thank you for extending your listing—we appreciate your confidence. Please be reassured that we are **doing** all that we possibly can to dispose of your property in what might be called a buyer's market. This year has produced a number of frustrations for the homeowner as well as for the real estate industry—from the highest mortgage interest rates in history to a current high unemployment rate.

We here at _____ Company are deeply committed to our challenging profession, and recognize the responsibility we have to you, our clients, in performing the tasks at hand.

With best regards and have a good day.

Sincerely,

4-15   LETTER REQUESTING A LISTING EXTENSION WHEN AN OFFER IS PENDING

Dear _____:

   In checking our records I find that the Listing Contract on your home at _____ Charles has expired. We have an offer pending so we will have to have a new contract signed. I have enclosed this new contract with an extension of 90 days, which will make the new expiration date June 16.

   I will appreciate your signature on the lines we have checked (x). Please return these contracts to me in the enclosed self-addressed envelope.

                              Yours truly,

4-16 ADJUSTING TERMS AND PRICE OF A LAND SALE

Dear _____:

Thank you for the new listing. I think you have made a wise decision in permitting us to sell the property in ½ acre portions.

I want to bring you up-to-date on the activity along _____ Street. Just recently, _____ Saving & Loan Company purchased 29,962 square feet of land on the south side of _____ Street next to the _____ on 90th & _____. They paid $1.95 a square foot for this ground. This property is in a better location than yours because it is near a major intersection.

I want to be very candid with you. I feel that your land is going to sell from $1.25 to $1.40 a square foot. That would be between $140,500 to $157,500. (You have 112,395 square feet.)

I will do all I can to obtain for you the highest possible price, but the property that _____ purchased is certainly a good comparable and, as I say, is better located than yours.

Sincerely,

4-17   LETTER AND QUESTIONNAIRE TO EXPIRED LISTING

Dear _____:

Thank you for allowing us to represent you in the sale of your property. We are sorry we were unable to consummate a sale for you.

We are constantly striving to give the finest services possible and your frank and personal comments about our service would be sincerely appreciated.

To make it quick and easy for you to answer, please use the reverse side of this letter. An envelope is enclosed for your convenience.

Thank you.

[REVERSE SIDE]

---

1. Did you receive the service you had expected? _____
   _____

2. Did our listing salesman keep you informed as to the showing activities on your property? _____ As to market conditions? _____

3. How many times did he contact you *in person* during the listing? _____ By phone call? _____

4. Has a member of our organization discussed with you the reasons why we feel your property didn't sell? _____

5. Please give us any suggestions or comments you would like to.

4-18 RELEASING SELLER FROM LISTING AGREEMENT

Dear _____:

In compliance with your request, we are hereby releasing you from the Listing Agreement dated _____, which was signed by you authorizing this office to sell the above-captioned property, owned by you.

This release is contingent upon the condition that should you sell the property within six months from the date hereof to anyone with whom this office has had negotiations, you shall be liable for commission to us at the rate of 7% of the sale price.

We sincerely regret that we were unable to consummate a sale for you, but should you feel that we can be of further service to you in any type of real estate, please do not hesitate to call upon us.

We wish to take this opportunity to thank you for the privilege of serving you.

Very truly yours,

4-19   COVER LETTER FOR SENDING PURCHASE AGREEMENT

Dear _____ :

Enclosed you will find the purchase agreement on your house at _____ So. 121 St. Please authorize the acceptance on the back and have it notarized. Please return the original and one copy as soon as possible so that we can proceed on closing your transaction.

We plan to close on May 3, and I will send you the necessary papers for your acknowledgement as soon as I know how you are holding title.

Thank you again for your confidence in our firm.

Sincerely yours,

4-20   SENDING PURCHASE AGREEMENT FOR AN OFFER BELOW THE LISTING PRICE

Dear _____ :

Please find enclosed a cash offer on your property at 335-337 _____ Street, ___(city)___ ___(state)___ .

I know this is not exactly what you are asking for, but this offer is cash. I am sure you could invest this money in another manner and make a better return (with fewer headaches) than you can with this property.

If you are in agreement with this offer, please sign it. Also, please have your wife sign. We will also need the abstract. Please send it to me.

Sincerely yours,

4-21   COVER LETTER FOR RELEASE AND AFFIDAVIT

Dear _____:

      Enclosed is the release that must be signed by you along with an affidavit which is required by the title company stating that _____ _____ and _____ _____ is one and the same person.

      Please have both instruments notarized and return them to me immediately. Thank you.

Sincerely,

AFFIDAVIT

      According to the records of the _____ County Court House in _____, _____, in book _____ of real estate mortgages, page _____, there is a mortgage from _____ _____ and _____ to _____ and _____ for Forty-Five Hundred Dollars (4,500.00) filed on November 1, _____. This affidavit states that _____ who with _____ secured a mortgage from _____ and _____ is one and the same person.

_____
_____

Subscribed and sworn to before me this _____ day of _____, 19_____.

_____
Notary Public

4-22   LETTER-AGREEMENT FOR REMOVAL OF CONTINGENCIES

Dear _____:

    Please be advised that the contingency clauses to sell property located at _____, Lot 13, Block 11, _____ District, ___(city),___ ___(state)___ are hereby removed and deleted from sales agreement dated March 27, 19__ to purchase property located at _____, Lot 13, Block 11, _____ District, _____, _____ by Miss _____, from Mr. _____ _____, Attorney in fact for _____ _____.

                                        _____
                                               Purchaser

_____   _____
        Witness   Purchaser

                                        _____
                                                 Seller

_____   _____
        Witness   Seller

4-23   LETTER-AGREEMENT FOR KEY TRANSFER

Dear _____:

   We do hereby agree that Mr. & Mrs. _____, purchasers of the property known as _____, _____, _____, may have the key for same on this date for purpose of _____.

   Mr. & Mrs. _____ will then become responsible for any damages that may occur to this property.

   Mr. and Mrs. _____ shall complete final settlement, as previously advised them, on Tuesday, October 18, 19__.

_____   _____(SEAL)
WITNESS

_____   _____(SEAL)
WITNESS

___ _____   _____(SEAL)
WITNESS

_____   _____(SEAL)

                                        Sincerely,

4-24   LETTER PREPARING THE SELLER FOR THE CLOSING

Dear _____:

Settlement for the above property will be held as follows:

Date: Hour:

Place:

The Title Company will require that you bring with you tax receipts for the following years: _____; and sewer receipts for: _____.

In addition, please bring any unpaid current tax bills to be adjusted between Seller and Buyer. *Cancelled checks will not be honored.* If you do not have all these receipts, please advise us IMMEDIATELY so that we may obtain tax certification from the Tax Collector's office.

We have requested a statement from your Mortgagee showing balance due to satisfy the existing mortgage, with directions to send to the Title Company with copy to you and copy to us.

Deed and Sellers' affidavit will be presented for your signatures at settlement; if for any reason you cannot be present, advise us at once so that we may obtain the signatures in advance.

An estimate of net proceeds due you is enclosed.

If there are any questions regarding these instructions or the enclosed statement, we urge you to telephone us for clarification.

Unless we hear to the contrary we shall be looking forward to seeing you as indicated herein.

Cordially yours,

4-25 COVER LETTER FOR CLOSING FORMS

Dear _____:

Thank you for your speedy reply on the purchase agreement. Enclosed you will find five items: 1. deed, 2. lien guarantee, 3. authorization form, 4. copy of original purchase agreement, and 5. note informing us that no other real estate company is involved.

Please sign the three forms as your name appears on the deed. Have the deed and the lien guarantee notarized.

We plan to close the sale of your home on Wednesday, May 3, __. Because the present insurance policy on your property is not a homeowner's policy, the purchaser is having a new policy written. You will receive back from your insurance agent a small proration.

Thank you again for your confidence in our firm.

Sincerely,

4-26 INSTRUCTIONS FOR COMPLETING CLOSING PAPERS

Dear _____:

The loan for Mr. _____ was approved today. We can close as soon as we receive the signed papers back from you. Please sign the deed and lien guarantee exactly as your name appears on the top of the deed. They must be notarized. On the back of these papers is a second notary form.

Enclosed is an extra copy of this letter to forward to Mr. _____, along with the deed, lien guarantee and authorization. As soon as your brother signs these instruments, please ask him to send them to me in the enclosed self-addressed envelope.

Sincerely,

4-27 MODEL LETTER EXPLAINING INTEREST CHARGES

Dear _____:

Thank you for the closing statement. In answer to your inquiry on the July interest debit of $71.89, at _____, as at many banks, the interest is paid in arrears. The July payment takes care of the June interest; the August payment pays the July interest, and so on. Since Mr. _____ makes the August payment, he was given credit for the July interest.

I hope this answers your question. It has been a pleasure to serve you. If I can be of further assistance, feel free to contact me.

Sincerely,

4-28   COVER LETTER RETURNING CLOSING PAPERS AND CHECK

Dear _____:

The closing of your home at _____ Street took place this morning. Enclosed are your closing papers and a check for $1,057.78. Please sign the copy of the closing statement and return it to us.

You are now free to obtain another FHA loan if you so desire. This credit report delayed closing until now.

It has been a pleasure working with you. If you have any questions, please contact me. Thank you.

Sincerely,

4-29   BROKER'S FOLLOW-UP TO SELLER AFTER THE SALE

Dear _____:

I am so glad that Mrs. _____ was able to help you sell your home.

She has told me how much she enjoyed working with you and I wanted to let you know that I appreciate the opportunity to have been of help.

Our success in the real estate business requires the continuous good will of all the people with whom we do business. I certainly hope that this selling experience has been a happy one and that when you are looking for property of any kind or are considering selling that you will call on us for assistance.

Sincerely yours,

4-30   MODEL LETTER: "PRIDE IS OUR PASSWORD"

Dear _____:

One of the regular themes we preach to our associates is the importance of pride. Pride in your performance, we tell them, is the key to our success in the real estate profession. We believe that the person who takes pride in the way his or her task is performed will produce a service others cannot duplicate.

We know you can obtain other real estate service elsewhere. BUT, do you get truly professional service? Our service and the execution of that service are the very best that the real estate profession is able to produce. We hope that our performance today has convinced you that pride has helped us to reach the goals of quality and service which we value so highly.

Sincerely,

4-31 THANK YOU LETTER AND QUESTIONNAIRE FOR THE SELLER

Dear _____:

We want to thank you for your cooperation in connection with the recent sale of your property. We always try to give the best possible service and sincerely trust that our sales personnel and office have served you satisfactorily. However, if, in your opinion, we fell short in any area, we certainly would appreciate it if you would let us know where you feel we could improve upon our service.

Now that your property is sold, we want you to know that we will continue to be interested in you, and want you to feel free to call upon us at anytime.

Wishing you every happiness in the future, I remain

Sincerely yours,

P.S. Enclosed you will find a questionnaire. I would appreciate your taking a few minutes of your time to fill it out and return it to me in the enclosed, stamped envelope. Thank you.

_____ ASSISTANCE QUESTIONNAIRE (for sellers)

DATE _____

ADDRESS _____

SALESPERSON _____

A) How did your contact with us originate?

____ a) Newspaper classified

____ b) Homes for Living

____ c) _____ Listing Magazine

____ d) Recommended by friend

____ e) Reputation of Company

____ f) Open House—Office

____ g) Other

B) *Evaluation: Always 10; Mostly 8; Sometimes 6; Occasion-ally 4; Never 2*

1. Was our salesperson courteous at
   all times?   _____

2. Was our salesperson knowledgeable
   about the property?   _____

3. Was our salesperson dependable?   _____

4. Was salesperson enthusiastic in his
   desire to serve you?   _____

5. Was our salesperson always neat in
   his appearance?   _____

6. Was our salesperson interested in
   your needs and wants?   _____

7. Was our salesperson punctual in
   keeping appointments?   _____

8. Was our salesperson helpful and honest in his negotiations between you as the seller, and the buyer? _____

9. Was our salesperson as conscientious and interested in assisting you with "follow up" and many details after the signed offer as he was before you signed? _____

10. When showing your home did our salesperson make a good presentation? _____

C) 1. Were you quoted the correct settlement charges? _____

2. How often during listing did salesperson counsel with you? _____

3. Did our salesperson make any personal promises that were not kept? _____

4. What were you most pleased and impressed with as far as _____ & Co. was concerned?

5. Were there any disagreements at the settlement table? _____

6. Would you recommend our company to your friends and relatives? (If answer is yes, please do so.) _____

7. Name of company or firm you are associated with. _____

8. Other Comments: _____

This entire survey to be completely confidential.

Thank you,

4-32 MOVING TIPS TO SELLER

Dear _____:

  Listed below are some moving tips. Before you leave your present address notify and or check on the following:

- Rubbish and garbage service
- Milk delivery
- Gas and Water—Metropolitan Utilities District
  Phone No. ____-____
- Shoes at repairman
- Electric Co.—_____ Public Power Phone # ____-
- Diaper Service
- Telephone Co. # ____-____
- Water Softener service
- Newspaper delivery
- Charge Accounts
- Have your refrigerator and other appliances serviced for the trip.
- Write the utility company in the city to which you are moving. Ask them about necessary fees or deposits required for installation of services.
- Remit the utility deposits requested, with information when and where you want the following services: Gas, Electric, Water & Telephone.
- Send your forwarding address to your local post office and send change of address cards to magazines, insurance companies, book clubs, friends and stores.
- Transfer your fire insurance on household goods or other insurance on personal possessions, so that they will be covered at your new home and en route.
- Notify the principal of your children's school about your intended move.
- Get letter from him covering the status of your children in school.

□ Notify the pastor of your church that you are leaving.
□ Obtain birth records, baptism records of all the children.
□ Get medical records, of shots, eyeglass prescription. (Have your doctor and dentist recommend men in your new hometown).
□ If car or other possessions are not paid for, get permission to move them.
□ Transfer your bank account.
□ Have your present bank arrange credit references for establishing new accounts in the city to which you are moving.
□ Arrange for sufficient cash or traveler's checks to cover the cost of moving services and expenses until you make banking connections in the city to which you are moving. Cash or certified check generally required to Transfer Co.

I hope these suggestions will be helpful to you.

Sincerely,

Chapter 5

Model Letters That Get
Potential Real Estate Buyers
Ready to Buy

Keeping in touch with your buyers, building rapport, handling
their objections and keeping the sales process moving ahead
smoothly and quickly are all subjects covered by the following
letters . . .

5-1 MODEL LETTER DESCRIBING A PERSONALIZED SALES PROGRAM

Dear _____:

      I certainly appreciate the opportunity of being YOUR REALTOR. I have a program that has been very successful in serving my purchasing clientele.

      The program is based on a thorough concentration of my efforts in securing a fine home for you. I work with only six purchasing clients at one time. By doing this, I am able to secure the right home for each.

      Please remember these points:

1. I appreciate the opportunity of being YOUR REALTOR.
2. I want to show you ANY HOME IN THE CITY—whether it is listed with our firm or another.
3. So please, let me do the work in securing your home. You will find that working with ONE REALTOR will make it easier for you to find a home. Permit me to thoroughly concentrate on securing you the HOME OF YOUR DREAMS.
4. If you should like to see an *open house*, please call me and I will arrange to show it to you. Once you give a salesman your name at an open house, you become his prospect. PLEASE CALL ME.

      Thank you for reading this letter, and again I welcome the opportunity of being YOUR REALTOR.

                    Sincerely,

5-2 LETTER STRESSING PROFESSIONAL GUIDANCE

Dear _____:

    The purchase of a home is one of the most important investments you will ever make. You need professional guidance from professional people to assist you in buying the right property.

A LARGE SELECTION AT A FULL RANGE OF PRICES

    We offer you a choice of many homes in all parts of _____ City. Our Multiple Listing Service enables us to meet your requirements, and to quickly locate the home you want. Every family is looking for a particular style in a particular price bracket. You tell us what you want and we will tell you where it is or we will locate it for you.

COMPLETE FINANCING

    Standard financing can be arranged through conventional, F.H.A., or G.I. loans. We often have attractive loan assumptions. To finance your DREAM HOUSE . . . call us today.

                              Sincerely,

5-3 FOLLOW-UP AFTER AN INQUIRY

Dear _____:

Thank you sincerely for inquiring about one of the properties we listed "For Sale."

We have many additional properties for sale. And as Realtors we have over 2,000 other listings in our files for you to choose from. These files contain pictures with information on all properties listed for sale by other Realtors in the city.

Most likely, in our listing files you and I can find the right home at the right price in the location you desire. I'd be happy to meet you at our office anytime.

For legal advice you need one competent lawyer.

For Real Estate advice you need *one competent Realtor*—Us!

Of course, you're under no obligation. Please call me again soon so we can get together. Thank you.

Sincerely yours,

5-4 OFFERING ASSISTANCE IN RELOCATING

Dear _____:

Good Morning! Good Afternoon! Good Evening!

No matter what time of day it is, I am ready to assist you in relocating. I sell for _____ Co., Realtors. We have been in business for over 26 years and your success in locating your new home is important to us.

We are members of Multiple Listing Service with hundreds of listings from which to choose. Our company has over 75 Exclusive Listings, both new and existing properties.

Enclosed is my card and some pictures of our listings. I would like to be of service to you. Please call soon.

Sincerely,

5-5 LETTER STRESSING THE NUMBER OF HOMES AVAILABLE—FOR NEWCOMERS

Dear _____:

Congratulations on planning a move to __(city),__ __(state__ . You'll find that our community is a picturesque place to live, and that your neighbors will be friendly and eager to welcome you.

_____ is situated at the foot of the _____ Mountains, which is like having your own private mountain in your back yard.

The selling and buying of homes here has been very active in the last three months. We have listed and sold more homes recently than we have ever done before in _____'s 15-year history. This activity is partially due to the stabilization of the interest rate on mortgages.

We, at _____ Real Estate, wish you a pleasant and smooth transition into _____. With the hundreds of listings that there are, let me be of assistance in the purchase of your new home.

Sincerely,

5-6 "WELCOME" LETTER WITH QUESTIONNAIRE—FOR NEWCOMERS

Welcome to _____! We'd like to know how you heard about our fine community, and why you are interested in looking for property here. Please take a few minutes to check off this questionnaire. This data will help us to establish priorities in our community efforts and support.

Heard about our city from _____
_____ a friend _____ a broker

Liked the description of:

_____ Country-suburb atmosphere

_____ Excellent schools

_____ One and two acre minimum zoning

_____ Cultural resources

_____ YMCA year round swim/recreation program

_____ Driving time to business

_____ Commuting (RR) time to business

_____ Price range of homes available

_____ Reasonable taxes in town

_____ tax advantages

_____ Good town government

_____ Newcomer's Club and other activities

_____ Friendly small town atmosphere

Thank you so much for helping us know what new residents like most about our fine city.

Sincerely yours,

5-7   LETTER DESCRIBING THE COMMUNITY TO NEWCOMERS

Dear _____:

    Mr. _____, a mutual friend of ours, asked me to get in touch with you and to send you some information about _____. You will find some brochures enclosed.

    _____ is a charming community of 16,500, located about 50 miles from _____ City. It is a setting of rolling, wooded hills, winding roads, old stone walls, and many streams and ponds. Much of the charm of our community is protected by the one and two acre minimum zoning. Our village offers convenient shopping in a pleasant and casual atmosphere, and there are many additional shopping centers nearby.

    The school system is considered excellent, and we are especially proud of our new high school which opened in 1971. There are many recreational facilities for children and adults such as a year-round recreation program, fine tennis courts, a community swimming pond, horseback riding, etc. There is a new Y with an olympic-sized swimming pool, paddle tennis courts, and a full program of activities.

    I have a number of homes to show you, and will look forward to helping you find one to fit your needs. Please let me know when you will be in this area. It will be a pleasure to meet you.

                      Sincerely,

5-8 ATTEMPTING TO OBTAIN A DEPOSIT QUICKLY

Dear _____:

It was certainly a pleasure meeting you and your lovely wife this morning. I am enclosing some information concerning _____ Ranches. The _____ school system does not have a brochure, but I can assure you it is a fine one.

I am enclosing an explanation of this school system which I typed up from a phone conversation I had this morning.

_____ Ranches represents a way of life to executives and their families, who enjoy country living close to a large metropolitan area. I can certainly see your family truly enjoying this location. As you stated while we were driving through _____ Ranches, it should not be a tough job to sell your daughter on the bridle trails in this area. There are 52 acres of horseback riding! It also appeared that your wife was very impressed by this style of home and the picturesque setting.

In closing I would like to make a recommendation to you, _____. No one ever knows the exact time when a home is going to sell. If we knew this, we could all be millionaires. I want to strongly suggest, therefore, that you place a deposit on this property as soon as possible. I would even suggest that you do this prior to your leaving town tomorrow.

I would be derelict in my duty to you as a client if I did not point out that this type of property could sell before you get back in town. I say this because two weeks ago 11 lots in _____ Ranches sold over the weekend. I do not want you to say to me 10 days from now, "Why didn't you push me!"

After reading over the enclosed information, please call me if you should have any questions.

Sincerely,

5-9   AN INVITATION TO A VISITOR

Dear _____:

    I am a close friend of John _____, a friend of your husband. He asked me to call and offer my services as a Realtor to you.

    When you are coming to _____, please give me a two or three day notice and I will arrange to show you some homes.

    I know you will enjoy _____, and I am looking forward to assisting you in finding a home.

Sincerely,

5-10   LETTER PROMPTING A BUYER TO BUY NOW

Dear _____:

    I know you mentioned to me the last time we talked that you would prefer to wait until Spring to make a move.

    We have an excellent home in the _____ area that is in your price range. I am enclosing the picture and information sheet pertaining to this fine home.

    I know you are busy in your work, but in many ways this is the best time of the year to move—moving companies are more available, prices of homes in some cases are somewhat softer, etc.

    Thank you for your past confidence in me, and let me know what your opinion is of this home.

Your friend,

5-11 HANDLING OBJECTIONS

Dear _____:

     Enclosed is the information that I said I would send you concerning the comparables I used in appraising _____ Smithe Ave.

     In answer to some of your questions: The leak in the ceiling would be corrected before anyone purchases this home. Mrs. _____ also mentioned that central air conditioning could be added to this home without too much difficulty. However, many times people prefer window units in two-story homes because of the difficulty in cooling the second floor. (The first floor is overly cool and the second floor is overly warm.) As far as the kitchen is concerned, the cost of alterations should not be too expensive because it is large and has quite adequate cupboards.

     This is a fine home and I feel you would be very happy there. Since I am leaving town for four days, I will contact you Friday. If you wish additional information while I am gone, please contact Mr. _____ of our office.

                                      Serviceably yours.

5-12 COVER LETTER FOR NEW MLS LISTINGS

Dear Friends:

Enclosed are a few of our listings that may interest you. You will see that some of these homes have other real estate broker's signs on them, since they are in our Multiple Listing Service. This means that the real estate brokers cooperate with each other in listing and selling them. With this cooperation, you can come in our office and see all the homes in the Southwest Suburban area offered for sale through the Multiple Listing Service.

If you would like to see these homes or possibly other homes we have listed, I will be glad to make an appointment for you.

I am enclosing my business card and would appreciate it very much if you would ask for me when you call or come into our office.

It will be a pleasure to be of service to you.

Sincerely,

5-13   OFFERING SERVICES TO A RETURNING FORMER RESIDENT

Dear _____:

I was talking to your father and he said you had been offered an excellent position here with your organization. This is certainly good news. He suggested that I write you a short note. I would certainly like to offer you and your wife our services in obtaining a suitable home when you move back to

_____

Please contact me by phone or letter and tell me what you are looking for and I will begin immediately to find a suitable home for your family.

Serviceably yours,

5-14 CONVEYING INFORMATION ABOUT PROPERTY TAXES

Dear _____:

   Thank you for sending back the information card. To answer your question about taxes, I would say that we are in the middle tax range. If you were to build a $40,000 home in the suburbs, your taxes would be approximately $1,200.00.

   Some additional information may be helpful to you. New houses are being built mainly in Southwest and Northwest _____. I feel that the greatest growth area today is in the Northwest.

   As to building your own home there are many nice suburban locations available and we are associated with a fine builder of custom homes. The interest rates are ranging from 7¾% to 8½% depending on the initial investment in a home.

   Whenever you plan to be in town, let me know and we can discuss the housing market completely. Thank you.

                              Serviceably yours.

5-15 THE PRO-AND-CON APPROACH TO GETTING A PROSPECT TO BUY

Dear _____:

   I know you really like the property on _____ Drive. To assist you, I am enclosing a *Why Letter*—a letter showing the pros and cons of a particular house. Please review this letter carefully.

                              Sincerely,

(Note: The following letter should be typed on a separate sheet of paper.)

WHY LETTER

TO: Mr. and Mrs. _____

Pros

Price $31,950 (Realistic)

To build today:

   1250 sq. ft. (approx)

   $20.00 sq. ft. with attached garage (depreciation for age deducted from sq. ft. cost)

   $25,000 (basic house & garage)

   $1,000 (air conditioning)

   $26,000

   $5,000 - $6,000 (lot)

   $31,000 - $32,000

Condition: basically very good

Location: very good (in this price range one of the finest in the city)

   1. schools—good, both public & parochial. (very definite resale point)

     a. Public—Dist. _____ finest in state

     (1) _____ 5 blocks- elementary

     (2) _____ 5 blocks- Junior High

     (3) _____ bus in front

Cons

Lot—a good large lot, but smaller backyard; with creative thinking something could be done— patio along side of house (many of these on side & front).

Floor dull—minor fault —some wax & elbow grease needed; woman sick that week, should have seen it before.

Slight split in block—no problem—small flaw in construction; this way when owner bought; no problems since.

Not a con, but a fact

   Normal depreciation —very little depreciation because of advancement of area in recent years— shopping, schools, transportation, recreation.

   Normal depreciation —2% per year.

   House 4 yrs. old.

Taxes—you get what you pay for—

Many say best school system in state.

Pros (Continued)

    (4) Excellent summer school program

    b. Parochial—St.

    _____ bus to school

2. Transportation—bus lines close
3. Shopping—very good
   - a. _____- 72nd & _____
   - b. _____- 73rd & _____
   - c. _____- 72 & _____
   - d. _____ _____- 1½ blocks
   - e. _____-_____ _____
4. _____ Country Club recreation & swimming pool _____ _____ Park - 78th & _____
5. Playground—1½ blocks away
6. All elements in buying a home here— Location, Price & Condition
7. Terrific house with fine basement—many possibilities in basement

    You may decide after studying this. I know you would be very happy with this home and this area.

                      Sincerely,

Chapter 6

Following Up On Buyers:
Model Letters That Can Get
You More Sales

Keeping in touch with your buyers, between the time an offer has been accepted and closed, and then following up after the close, will assure you of more sales and of more prospects for the future. Here are 27 model letters that will enable you to do this effectively and easily . . .

6-1 MODEL LETTER FOR COMPLETION OF PURCHASE AGREEMENT

Dear _____:

Congratulations on the purchase of the home on _____ Drive! You and your family will certainly enjoy this fine home.

On the front page of the purchase agreement, I will need your name as you wish it to appear on the deed. Also, on the front page I will need your initials on the far left side of paragraphs 2 & 5. On the back side, I will need your initials right above where Mrs. _____ has signed her name. Also, initial the typed portion where it states that you will close on June 1, with possession on July 1st.

Please inform me about the following three items:

1. The name of your attorney, so that I can take the contract and have it approved by him on or before April 25.
2. Let me know when you can accompany the tradesmen and myself to obtain a firm bid on the addition to be built. This must be done by April 25.
3. Also, by April 25 I must receive from you an additional $1,000 as an earnest deposit.

Thank you very much _____, for your confidence in me.

Sincerely,

6-2   GETTING THE BUYER READY FOR THE CLOSING

Dear _____:

Congratulations! You have just signed a contract to purchase your new home and we are happy to have been able to help you with your selection.

The contract form that you signed was approved by both the _____ Bar Association and the Board of Realtors. You probably are familiar with the Standards for Real Estate transactions (on the reverse side), however, we would like to call your attention to the following:

A.   SURVEY. There may be an existing survey, but this is your responsibility and may be required for your financing.

B.   TERMITE INSPECTION. You have the right to have the property inspected by the exterminator of your choice and at your expense.

C.   PERSONAL PROPERTY. The appliances and machinery should be inspected within the required time period and, if necessary, an objection filed within five days prior to closing.

D.   PROCEEDS OF SALE. The money required at closing should be either cash, cashier's, certified or Savings & Loan Assn. check drawn on local funds.

There are various companies that do the above mentioned work and, although we do not recommend any specific company, we will be happy to work with the companies of your choice, making arrangements for their inspection.

We also recommend that you use an attorney to close your transaction and obtain an opinion of title or title insurance from either your attorney or a title company.

In addition, we would like to remind you that the information on our listing form is believed to be correct and factual, but is not warranted or guaranteed by our office. The information has been received from sources that we feel are reliable, including the seller, but we suggest that you take the time to verify this information to your own satisfaction.

　　　If you have any questions about these or any items pertaining to this transaction, please feel free to call on us.

Sincerely,

6-3 LETTER-AGREEMENT FOR SELL-BACK

Dear _____:

In the event _____, Realtors purchases a certain property described as:

_____

_____

under the terms of a certain guarantee to purchase agreement executed on even date herewith, _____, Realtors guarantees to sell back to the Owners the above Realty described property at a figure of $_____ LESS than the amount paid by _____, Realtors under the aforementioned agreement.

Date _____   Sincerely,

By _____

6-4 MODEL LETTER SUGGESTING INTERIM FINANCING

Dear _____:

It was nice visiting with you Wednesday. I hope you had success over the weekend in selling your property, but if you didn't, I certainly would not worry. You have a very saleable property, and I can assure you that it will sell.

The weather has been outstanding in _____, and I know you want to begin working on the property you purchased there _____, as soon as you can.

In our phone conversation, _____, we talked about interim financing. It appears to me that this might be the best route to follow in your transaction. You are certainly in a fine position for this type of financing to work. The reasons I say this are:

1. You have a fine property in _____ that apparently is quite saleable.
2. You have a large equity in your property.
3. You have purchased an excellent property in _____, which will meet your and your family's needs. Seldom can one make such an outstanding purchase close to a large metropolitan area.

With all of these pluses you should be able to obtain interim financing with no trouble at all from your banker in _____. In simple terms, you borrow what you need against the equity in your present property. You can pay this loan back when you sell your property. These loans can generally be negotiated on an interest-only basis or set up on a monthly payment schedule that will blend in with your budget. By doing this, you can close the transaction on the property in _____ and begin working on it.

Interim financing is used all the time and I have never had it place a bind on the purchaser. In fact, I have negotiated interim financing for two clients during the past month and both have been very happy with this avenue of financing.

If you have any further questions, please call me.

Sincerely,

6-5   COVER LETTER FOR RENTAL STATEMENT TO BUYER AWAITING LOAN APPROVAL

Dear _____:

Enclosed is rental statement on _____ Hamilton. Rent will be from August 8 to September 8, 19___.

Don't give up, the 235 money is coming, but I am not sure when.

The owner asked if you would mow the front yard. If you are not able to find someone, let me know and I will see that it is done. Thank you.

Sincerely,

6-6   TAX INFORMATION TO THE BUYER

Dear _____:

Enclosed is a copy of the GI appraisal plus a copy of the purchase agreement. The homeowner is the only one able to get an adjustment on taxes. This must be done by March 1, 19___. Perhaps you could call the _____ Co. and they could advise you if it could be done through the mail. Their telephone number is _____.

As regards the January 1 taxes, they become delinquent April 1, 19___.

I hope this information will be helpful to you in getting a tax adjustment.

Sincerely,

6-7 NOTICE THAT ANOTHER OFFER WILL BE ACCEPTED

Dear _____:

    We wish to take this opportunity to thank you for your contract to purchase our property known as _____, dated _____.

    Under the terms of the contract, we accepted a contingency clause concerning the sale of your property located at _____, on or before settlement of your new home above mentioned.

    We are, therefore, giving you 72 hours notice on our intentions to accept another contract on our property above-mentioned and unless you are willing to remove the contingency clause therein contained, our agreement of sale with you will become null and void 72 hours from date and time recorded below.

                          Sincerely,

6-8 NOTE SUGGESTING INSURANCE COVERAGE

Dear _____:

Mrs. _____ has informed me that you are welcome to store any items in the second garage during the Christmas holidays.

You will need an insurance policy at closing, and these items will be fully covered by a Homeowners Policy that we can write. A $15,000 Homeowners Policy with good and adequate protection would cost _____ per year. If this is satisfactory to you, we will write the policy at the closing.

We are preparing closing papers and will send them to you as soon as possible.

Sincerely,

6-9 COVER LETTER FOR OFFER ACCEPTANCE

Dear _____:

Enclosed is the acceptance of the offer of $30,500 on _____ South 76th Street. Note the reverse side of the contract. The seller also mentioned that if any repairs such as painting, are required by F.H.A., these will be your responsibility. I don't feel that the F.H.A. will require this because the paint is not in bad condition.

_____ Savings and Loan Association will send you the necessary loan papers. I will see Mr. _____ this afternoon and instruct him on this. Thank you.

Sincerely,

6-10   COVER NOTE FOR MORTGAGE COMMITMENT

Dear _____:

     We enclose a copy of the firm commitment for your mortgage which we received today from _____ Mortgage Company.

     If we can be of any further assistance, please contact Mr. _____ at our office.

                 Very truly yours,

6-11   OFFERING ASSISTANCE ON INSURANCE

Dear _____:

As we have discussed, the mortgage company requires a one year paid insurance policy when you complete the transaction. Because of the appreciation of real estate values, we are recommending a coverage slightly higher than your mortgage. Also we will study the appreciation factor of your home on a yearly basis and recommend changes in your coverage if necessary. These changes must meet with your approval, of course.

Enclosed is the form prepared by us showing the amount of coverage we recommend for your new home. For comparison, the annual premium for a $30,000 Form III Homeowner's Policy with the company we represent would be $141.00.

_____ Co. is a fine organization, noted for its excellent claim service. My own home is insured by them and I have been quite satisfied with them.

If I can be of any assistance, please call me.

Your friend,

6-12   INSTRUCTIONAL LETTER PRIOR TO CLOSING

Dear _____:

Enclosed are photocopies of the Certificate of Real Estate Deed Transfer, the Warranty Deed, the Mortgage Statement and the Affidavit. Mr. _____, your attorney, told me to mail these to you. Also, enclosed is an assignment and transfer of stock shares to the _____ Savings and Loan and a copy of the closing statement. Return these two with your check.

Please return the check for $7,561.70 to Mr. _____, _____ National Bank Bldg, _____, _____, _____ by Friday, June 18, 19___. Make the check payable to the _____ Real Estate Company.

If you have any questions, please call me. Mr. _____ and I will represent you at the Friday closing.

Your insurance policy has arrived and I will send it to you Friday with a bill enclosed. Thank you.

Sincerely,

6-13 NOTICE OF CLOSING PLACE AND DATE

Dear _____:

The closing of your mortgage is set for 2 P.M. on Monday, July 5, 19___. It will take place at _____ Savings & Loan located on _____ and _____ Streets.

Enclosed is an estimate of the closing costs. You will be required to present the sum of $_____ by certified check, made payable to the Title Company noted above, which sum represents the difference between the purchase price and the mortgage being created, less the sum paid on account.

The settlement charges may be paid by your personal check at the time of settlement.

We look forward to seeing you, and want to thank you again for having us represent you in this transaction.

Cordially yours,

6-14 COVER LETTER FOR CLOSING PAPERS

Dear _____:

    Enclosed are all the closing papers for you to have examined by your attorney. We have set December 10th as the closing date. We will need a check from you for $2,873.04 by this date, so that we can have Mrs. _____ sign papers. We will file the deed and return it to you. The contract states possession to be 45 days after closing, which would mean January 25th. Mrs. _____ has paid rent up to the 10th of January. She is anxious to move also, and will try to be out sooner than the 25th.

    Please sign the Credit Information Statement for _____ Mortgage Company, and the Real Estate Transfer Statement. Please sign the Purchaser Closing Statement and return the 2nd copy to us. The Deed, Lien Guarantee and the Assignment papers are to be returned also.

    If there are any questions, please call us. Thank you.

                                     Sincerely,

6-15 LETTER REQUESTING REFERRALS, AFTER THE CLOSING

Dear _____:

We have recently had the pleasure of assisting you in the selection and purchase of your newly acquired home and we sincerely hope the entire transaction was handled to your complete satisfaction.

For most people, buying a home is one of the more important events in their family's life. We appreciate the confidence you displayed in allowing us to handle this sale for you. We sincerely hope that you will be pleased with your new home and that it will afford you many years of happiness.

Our service goes BEYOND THE CONTRACT and really never ends. We would like you to look upon us as your Real Estate Counselors and never hesitate to call upon us for advice in connection with your property or any real estate matter.

It goes without saying, of course, that I would appreciate your recommending me and our office to any of your friends.

With kind personal regards, we remain

Sincerely yours,

6-16 MODEL LETTER OFFERING ADDITIONAL SERVICES TO BUYER

Dear _____:

I am so glad that Mr. _____ was able to help you find the home of your choice.

He has told me how much he has enjoyed working with you in this selection. I wanted to let you know that I appreciate the opportunity to have been of help.

Our success in the real estate business requires the continuous good will of all the people with whom we do business. I certainly hope that this buying experience has been a happy one and that when you are looking for property of any kind or are considering selling, you will call on us for assistance.

Sincerely yours,

6-17   COVER NOTE FOR "TREE OF GOLD" COUPON

Dear _____:

It has been a distinct pleasure for us to assist you with your choice of a new home. Mr. _____ and I thank you for giving us the opportunity to be of service and for your fine cooperation throughout. Should you have any questions concerning this transaction, please call us.

We are enclosing a coupon which entitles you to a "Tree of Gold," which has been named the official tree of _____. If you will present this coupon to _____ Nursery, they will be happy to assist you with your selection of a tree and advise you as to planting and care.

Best wishes are extended for your future happiness in your new home.

Sincerely yours,

6-18 OFFER OF FUTURE SERVICE TO BUYER

Dear ———————:

Thank you for permitting our office to negotiate the purchase of your new home.

We certainly wish you and your family the best of all good things in the years ahead and may your life in your new home be full and happy.

Through the years we've become more and more grateful to the folks we do business with. We believe your home is a most important part of your life and that of your family. Your happiness in it is essential to your success and is important to us.

We want you to know that our willingness to be of service does not cease now that you have signed all the papers. Feel free to contact us any time we can be of help. We will always value the privilege of serving as your Realtor.

Sincerely yours,

6-19 MODEL LETTER OFFERING ADDITIONAL SERVICES TO BUYER

Dear _____:

We sincerely hope that all the details on the purchase of your home were handled to your complete satisfaction.

It is our aim to handle sales in such a manner that we merit your confidence and good will. It has always been an inspiration for us to have customers return for our help as their needs change and to have them refer their friends to us.

We are equipped to serve you in many ways. In addition to selling real estate, we operate a mortgage loan department, handle rentals, and do a substantial amount of appraisal work. Should you ever require assistance in these areas, please feel free to get in touch with us.

May we take this opportunity to wish you years of happiness in your new home.

Sincerely yours,

6-20 ANNIVERSARY LETTER TO THE PURCHASER

Dear _____:

    We are writing this to you hoping that you will receive it on your anniversary.

    Today is the anniversary of the actual closing of the purchase of your home. You now have owned it for ___ years. We hope that your home has been a source of much happiness for you and your family and that it will continue to be in the years to come.

    As we said after the sale was concluded, our service goes BEYOND THE CONTRACT and really never ends. We remain interested and want you to feel free to call upon us at any time if we can be of assistance to you.

    With kind regards and hoping you and yours enjoy many more happy years in your home, we remain

                    Yours very truly,

6-21   LETTER TO A "LOST" CUSTOMER

Dear _____:

I would like to take this opportunity to wish you and your family every happiness in the home you have recently purchased.

Naturally, I am sorry that I was unable to secure a home suitable for you, however, I do appreciate the opportunity you allowed me in trying to find the right home for you.

I sincerely hope that if you or any of your friends have any real estate questions or problems that I will be called.

Again, wishing you every happiness and trusting you will not hesitate to call or stop by any time, I remain with kind regards,

Sincerely yours,

6-22   HOMESTEAD EXEMPTION REMINDER

Dear _____:

Just a reminder to let you know that to take advantage of the Homestead Exemption on your property taxes you must file before April 1, _____.

If you have not already done so, please take your General Warranty Deed, Car Registration and Voter's Registration to the Tax Assessor's Office, which is located one-half block South of _____.

We appreciate the opportunity to have handled your real estate transaction during the past year.

If we can assist you in any of your real estate needs, please feel free to call us.

Sincerely,

6-23 LETTER TO THE BUYER OF A CUSTOM-BUILT HOME

Dear _____:

We have completed the seeding of the lawn on your new home. We are all pleased with the wonderful cooperation and patience you had during its construction. Sharing the building of the home with you was a pleasant experience. Of course, we wish you happiness and good living for many years to come.

I am enclosing your Warranty on the house. Please read it carefully before you put it away. Should you encounter any problems, please call us.

At this point, I would like to ask a favor of you. I am enclosing twelve of my business cards; I would like you to carry them with you, should you hear of anyone interested in building, buying or selling, please give him one of the cards. Be sure to tell them to say you sent them. Thanks very much.

Sincerely yours,

6-24 COVER NOTE FOR DEED

Dear _____:

Enclosed is the Deed to your new house. This is the Warranty Deed and has been recorded as stated on the bottom of the Deed. I would suggest that you keep this with your valuable papers. It has been recorded at the County Court House.

I will advise you as soon as the occupants move.

Sincerely,

6-25 NOTE ON POSSESSION DATE

Dear _____:

I checked with the present tenants of your new home this morning and they informed me that they will be moving out on August 29th or 30th. We thought it would be the 25th, but they cannot get possession of their home until the 29th and technically they have, as tenants, until September 1, 19___.

I also checked with District 66 Schools and was told that school opens September 2nd, and that you go to the school personally to register your children. Just let me know if I can provide further assistance.

Sincerely,

6-26   COVER NOTE FOR WARRANTY DEED

Dear _____:

It is a pleasure for us to send the Warranty Deed for the property which you purchased recently at _____ N. Oak. Please note that the Deed has been properly recorded at the court house and you may file it away for safekeeping. We are enclosing a folder that we hope you will find useful for your legal papers.

We are most appreciative that you chose _____ Realty to assist with your real estate needs and we hope that you will think of us in the future if you or any of your friends need advice on real estate. Thank you.

Sincerely,

6-27 MOVING-IN TIPS FOR THE NEW HOMEOWNER

Dear _____:

Listed below are some moving-in tips you might find helpful at your new address:

1. Check on service of telephone, gas, electricity, water, fuel for furnace.
2. Have your stove serviced—check pilot light.
3. Check pilot light on hot water heater, incinerator and furnace.
4. Have refrigerator, washer, television set checked.
5. Ask mailman for mail he may be holding for your arrival.
6. Have new address recorded on driver's license.
7. Visit city offices and register for voting.
8. Register car within five days after arrival in state or a penalty may have to be paid when getting new license plates.
9. Register family in your new place of worship.
10. Register children in school.
11. You should call the county Assessor's Office and make out the appropriate Homestead Exemption Application so that you can save some real estate taxes on your property. Phone No.

_____

I certainly hope you find these helpful.

Sincerely,

Chapter 7

Model Letters to Real Estate
Lessees and Lessors

Included in this chapter are 27 model letters covering just about
all aspects of the relationship between landlord, tenant and real
estate agent . . .

7-1 RENTAL LETTER—AGREEMENT—WHILE MORTGAGE IS BEING PROCESSED

Dear _____:

It is hereby agreed and understood by the parties hereto, being seller and purchasers of property located at _____ Ayres Street, _____, _____, that the purchasers of subject property hereby agree to accept this property as complete in every detail and do agree to complete final settlement for the purchase thereof immediately upon being advised that the mortgage papers are in proper form for their signatures.

They do further agree to pay the sum of Three Dollars ($3.00) per day, effective date of occupancy, for early possession and to continue to pay the sum of Three Dollars ($3.00) per day for each day they continue to occupy this property until final date of settlement.

It is further agreed that if purchasers fail to make settlement when notified, all deposit monies will be forfeited, and all the terms of the Agreement of Sale shall become null and void.

Very truly yours,

_____   _____
Witness

_____   _____
Witness

_____   _____
Witness

7-2   LETTER TRANSMITTING ESSENTIAL PROPERTY
INFORMATION CONCERNING THE SHARING OF SPACE

Dear _____:

   I certainly appreciate the opportunity of talking with you yesterday concerning your office needs. As you mentioned, you do not need a lot of space for your operation. Because we have more space than we need now, we could offer you the opportunity of sharing our office at a very competitive rate. Small office areas in good locations are difficult to find. I feel that my proposal would meet your needs and afford you one of the finest locations in _____.

   The space we talked about this morning is as follows:

Address: _____ Bedford St.

Square Footage: 700

Rent including utilities: $235 per month

Leases: Until June 1, 19___, and then options on a 1 year basis.

   The office is carpeted and draped. There is a conference room in the 700 square feet. If you so desired, we would share this room at a reduced rent.

   If this proposal interests you, please contact me and we will arrange a meeting to discuss the matter.

                                        Sincerely,

7-3 MODEL LETTER STRESSING CONTINUED SERVICE

Dear _____:

Thank you for calling me concerning the office space at _____. I am sorry it doesn't meet your needs.

I will continue to look for a suitable location for you. As I mentioned on the phone, I can show you any property whether we have it listed or another company has it listed. So, if you see something that I may miss, I would appreciate your calling me.

I welcome the opportunity to be your Realtor.

Sincerely,

7-4 LETTER DESCRIBING PROPERTY FOR LEASE

Dear _____:

Thank you for calling me. I want to inform you of the fine office space we have for lease for one of our clients. This space would be excellent for a general practioner of dentistry or medicine—particularly for one who is just beginning his practice. It would afford you the opportunity of having an excellent location with a minimal amount of rent. Some of the high points concerning this space are:

1. Location

   _____ Maple Street (directly behind _____ Pharmacy)

   High traffic and business area (_____ Pharmacy, _____ Food, etc.)

2. 4,000 square feet available (This can be broken down into smaller units)

3. Lease rates are very competitive

   $2.15 per square foot (1st year)

   $3.20 per square foot (2nd through 5th year)

4. What is provided:

   a. Shell Furnace and air conditioning (duct work is the responsibility of the tenant—one year free maintenance on these two).

   b. Wiring is provided to the electric box.

   c. This building was constructed with fine material and workmanship.

When you visit _____ _____ concerning this matter, please call me and I will make arrangements to show you this fine location.

Sincerely,

7-5 COVER NOTE AND LISTING AGREEMENT

Dear _____:

Please have your attorney approve this agreement, return it to me and we will consummate the transaction.

THIS AGREEMENT made by and between _____, party of the first part, and _____ Co., Realtor, a _____ Corporation, party of the second part:

WHEREAS the party of the first part is desirous of securing a lease for the building at _____, which is the building formerly occupied by _____,

THEREFORE it is agreed that the party of the first part, in consideration of the agreement of the party of the second part to list and offer for lease this property, give the sole and exclusive right until February 1, 19____, to lease the above designated property on the following terms subject to the approval of the first party:

Lease-rental shall be $750.00 per month.

Term of the lease shall be 10 years with a one 5 year renewal option.

Credit of prospective lessee shall be subject to approval of the party of the first part.

If a lease is made before the expiration of this listing by the party of the first part or any other person, on terms acceptable to the party of the first part, said party of the first part will pay to the party of the second part a commission of five (5%) per cent of the gross rental for the first 10 years provided in the lease.

In case of the forfeiture, by a prospective lessee, of any earnest money payment upon the within described property, said earnest money, after expense incurred to date has been deducted, shall be divided equally between the parties hereto, in proportions of one-half to the party of the first part and one-half to the party of the second part.

The commission schedule on this lease, between
_____, party of the first part, and _____ Co.,
Realtor, a _____ Corporation, party of the second
part, will be as follows:

One-fourth (¼) of the commission will be payable at the
time when the lessee signs the lease.

One-fourth (¼) in one year from the signing of the lease.

One-fourth (¼) in a year and one-half (18 months) from the
signing of the lease.

The final one-fourth (¼) in two (2) years from the signing of
the lease.

If, after the first ten (10) years, the option for the additional
five (5) years is renewed, the commission will be payable as
follows:

One-half (½) at the time the lessee signs the lease.

One-half (½) in one year from the signing of the lease. The
commission on the renewal 5 year option will be 3% (three per
cent).

_____

_____

Party of the first part

_____ Co., Realtor

By _____

Party of the second part.

7-6 AUTHORIZATION LETTER FOR AGENT TO SEEK LEASE PROPERTY

Dear _____:

This letter will outline the method by which I will assist you in the purchase or lease of the real estate in the City of _____ for the purpose of _____.

I am pleased, in consideration of this agreement, to use my best efforts for the purchase or lease and to accept the exclusive right as your exclusive agent and solely as your representative for the purchase or lease of such property on the following terms and conditions:

1. I am authorized to negotiate and submit the offer to purchase or lease and/or obtain options to purchase or lease the described property at prices to be approved by you in advance and/or on such other terms and conditions as may be acceptable to you, provided, however, that all of the terms and conditions are reviewed and approved by your attorney and/or accountant. It is understood that you shall have the right to reject any sales offers or lease offers to you through me without obligations or liabilities to you to me or from the prospective sellers or lessors.

2. If I solicit or actively engage the cooperation of any other real estate brokers, agents or other individuals, any compensation due them or claimed by them shall be my sole obligation and liability. I agree to prepare, evaluate, compare and provide you information about the potential purchase or lease of any real estate without any service fee, except as otherwise provided hereunder.

3. You will pay me a brokerage fee of 7% of the purchase price or 7% of the gross lease fee for all of my services in connection with the purchase or lease of the real estate by you covered hereunder. The fee will be payable to me only on closing of the purchase or lease.

In the event that any of the property is purchased or leased or optioned to purchase or optioned to lease by you which is covered under this agreement within 90 days after the date of termination of this agreement, you will pay me a broker's fee of 3½% of the purchase price or 3½% of the gross lease fee of said property.

4. You agree to pay me as compensation for obtaining the option an amount equal to 3½% of the purchase price or lease price covered in the option agreement as my fee, which payment will apply toward my brokerage fee if the option is picked up and the purchase or lease is completed.

5. During the period in which this agreement is in effect, I will submit to you all inquiries regarding any real estate available in accordance with your requirements hereunder, and I will submit to you in writing all offers for the sale or lease of the property of which I have information.

6. This agreement will commence immediately and terminate on December 31, 19___, unless extended in writing by both parties. Within ten (10) days after termination, I will forward to you a list of the names and addresses of any prospects whom I reasonably think are likely to sell and my information as to their terms of sale.

7. Any compensation received by me as a result of the purchase or lease of this property from any other corporation, partnership, organization, or individual shall be offset against any fees or compensation due from you.

The foregoing being acceptable to you, will you please sign and return to me the duplicate original of this letter which is enclosed.

Very truly yours,

By _____
　　Commercial-Industrial Broker
　　(Salesman)

7-7   LETTER AND FORM FOR COMMISSION TO SALES ASSOCIATE

Dear _____:

      Please complete this form immediately upon execution of lease. Obtain your manager's approval and give a copy to the secretary for processing.

PROPERTY: _____TENANT: _____

SQUARE FEET: _____ RATE: $_____ PER SQ. FT. PER YR.

TERM OF LEASE: _____GROSS AMOUNT OF LEASE: $_____

AGREED COMMISSION: _____

TOTAL COMMISSION DUE: $ _____

COMMISSION DISBURSEMENT

DUE_____ BOARD OF REALTORS: $ _____
_____: SALES ASSOCIATE_____ $_____
           SALES ASSOCIATE_____ $_____
           OFFICE $_____
TOTAL COMMISSION PAID $_____
COMMISSION CHECK RECEIVED: _____ DISBURSED: _____

SIGNATURES:
                        APPROVED BY
ASSOCIATE_____, _____MANAGER _____

                              Sincerely,

7-8 MEMO TO TENANTS ON LAWN CARE

To: Tenants   Date _____

From: Property Manager

    The owners of _____ Apartments make every effort to keep the lawns in a condition that will compliment the care that is given lawns by homeowners in the vicinity. Please assist us in keeping the lawns in good condition by asking your children to refrain from playing on them.

    Thank you for your co-operation.

MEMO TO TENANTS ON NOISE LEVELS

To: Tenants   Date _____

From: Property Manager

    During a recent inspection in _____ we noticed that there was a stereo being played at a loud volume.

    We ask the co-operation of all of our tenants in observing the rules of the apartment building by not playing radios, T.V.'s, stereos, etc., too loudly or too late in the evening. Undue noise of any kind makes it difficult on other tenants. Since we have always had the utmost co-operation of our tenants, we are sure that this problem can be resolved quickly.

    Thank you, and best wishes for the coming holidays.

7-10   MEMO TO TENANTS ON HANDLING OF TRASH

To: Tenants   Date _____

From: Property Management Department

  Recently we have had calls from some of the men who do work for our company in and around your apartments pointing out a few problems that exist. Since we feel that our tenants do take pride in their homes, we would like to pass these comments on to you.

  The new dumpsters have added to the neat appearance of _____. Help us to keep them attractive and odorless by always placing your trash in plastic bags before putting it out for collection.

  Basements are a part of your home. Please be sure that anything belonging to you is placed in your storage bin. Anything not in a bin will be removed and the tenant will be billed for removal. Empty cartons, etc., should be removed. In cleaning the basements recently, it was noted that there is a great deal of cat litter in the basements. Pets are not permitted in _____. Anyone having a pet is in violation of his lease and can be given notice to vacate.

  So many of you have been inconvenienced by water in your basements. Did you know that almost all of this was caused by paper towels, Pampers, and tampons? These items were removed from the drains by our plumbers. Please be careful in disposing of these. A nylon hose on the end of your washer hose will prevent lint from clogging the drain.

  If everyone follows these suggestions, we are sure that you will agree and it will make the _____ apartments an even better place to live. Thank you for the co-operation you have always shown.

7-11   MEMO TO TENANTS ON PLUMBING REPAIRS

To: Tenant   Date _____

From: Property Manager

_____ Plumbers will be in _____ on Tuesday, January 18, 19___ to make some necessary repairs.

We would appreciate it if you could arrange to let the plumber into your apartment since he does not carry a pass key.

If you wish to contact him, his number is _____.

Your co-operation would be appreciated.

7-12 MODEL LETTER TO CONDOMINIUM TENANTS ON RULES OF CONDUCT

Dear _____ Resident:

Enclosed please find new rules to be added to the Rules of Conduct applicable to all residents in the _____ condominiums. At the time you signed your lease, you should have received a copy of the Rules of Conduct. If, for some reason, you did not receive a copy of the rules, please contact your landlord and request one.

We hope you are enjoying living in _____ and are sure you can see the reasons for all residents abiding by the Rules of Conduct.

Perhaps at some time in the future, you will decide you would like to become a homeowner of one of our condominiums. We would like to have you as one.

Sincerely,

Rules of Conduct

I. Vehicles

(a) Automobiles and any other permitted vehicles shall be parked only within the painted lines of a designated parking area. No vehicle shall park, stop or stand along the side or in the middle of any entrance or exit driveway; or within a parking area so as to impede or prevent ready access to and from any other vehicle or parking space. No inoperable or unlicensed vehicle shall be parked within the condominium project for more than forty-eight (48) hours. The condominium council shall have the right to cause any vehicle not conforming with these regulations to be moved or towed away, as necessary, at the offending unit owner's expense, and without liability for damage caused to the moved or towed vehicle.

(b) All parking regulations posted or promulgated by the condominium council from time to time for the safety, comfort and convenience of the owners shall be strictly obeyed.

(c) No unit owner or occupant shall cause or permit the blowing of any horn, or screeching of any tires, from any vehicle in which his family, tenants, employees, guests or invitees shall be passengers or drivers, approaching or upon any of the driveways or parking areas serving the project, except as may be required for the safe operation of such vehicle.

(d) No vehicle shall be repaired, tuned, or otherwise mechanically serviced or attended (except for such emergency measures as changing flat tires) on the condominium project.

II. Ground and Walks

(a) The Council's maintenance responsibilities for grounds and walks shall include grass cutting, snow removal, pavement repair, watering, pruning, trimming, edging, raking, and sweeping of sidewalks and litter pick-up. No unit owner or occupant therefore shall till, seed, plant, cultivate, roll, cut trim, edge, water, fertilize, or otherwise treat the land or plantings thereon, or cause or permit same to be done, except in accordance with the instructions issued from time to time by Council, or, in the absence of applicable instructions, except with the Council's permission. Nor shall any unit owner or occupant cause or permit any walks to be salted, wetted, obstructed, or used other than for ingress and egress, except as may be otherwise permitted or directed by instructions of Council. Each unit owner, occupant, employee and guest shall refrain from littering the common areas.

(b) No signs, lampposts, additional fences other than those provided by Owner/Developer, birdbaths, or other improvements or adornments shall be erected or placed upon the lands of the project except pursuant to the Council's unanimous written permission. No existing fences or enclosures, walks, or curbs shall be painted, written or drawn upon, used to mount a sign, removed, marked or otherwise defaced. Lawn chairs, tables, barbecues, game equipment and other such items shall be placed upon the grounds only at such times and places as Council may from time to time prescribe; and shall be removed from the grounds when not in use unless otherwise permitted in writing by Council. No unenclosed common area, whether limited or not, shall be used for the unsightly storage of bicycles, sleds, baby carriages, baby pens, lawn furniture, ladders, tools, toys, or any other articles of whatever nature, without the written consent of Council.

(c) No fires shall be caused or permitted in the grounds, except for the lighting of gas or coal in an elevated, safe, enclosed grill used in the proper area. No activity shall be carried on upon the grounds which will cause unreasonable wear and tear to the grounds or damage to the landscaping.

(d) All garbage and other refuse shall be kept out of sight in tightly covered, water-proof containers. Each unit owner or occupant shall take all reasonable steps to prevent such containers and the contents thereof from emitting odors sufficient to reasonably annoy any adjacent unit owner or occupant. This provision shall not apply to location of dumpsters.

III. Pets

Dogs, cats, and other ambulatory pets shall, when not on a leash, be kept within a unit or confined to the limited common area serving the pet owner's unit. No dog, cat, or other animal shall be permitted to relieve itself on any shrub, fence or car. Any solid waste left on any common area, shall be promptly placed in a bag and placed in the pet owner's refuse container. Every pet owner shall take all reasonable steps to prevent the noise, waste, or odors of his pet from annoying other unit owners. Unit owners and occupants shall be strictly liable for the actions of same. The Council shall have the right to require that any habitually diseased, infested, unclean or noisy animal, reptile or fish be removed from the condominium project.

IV. Townhouse and Apartment Exteriors

(a) No unit owner or occupant shall cause or permit any sign to be displayed on or from, or any rug, laundry, fan, wire or other object to hang or protrude from any window or door. All draperies shall be lined with a white or off-white liner. All screens or screening not installed by the Developer shall be subject to the Council's written approval as to appearance, design, materials and manner of installation. No shades, awnings or window guards shall be used except with the Council's written approval. No sign or other object shall be displayed on any wall or rooftop without the Council's written approval.

The foregoing shall not prohibit the display of customary holiday decorations, subject to such specific limitations on type, manner of display, and duration as the Council may from time to time fix and determine.

(b) No rugs shall be beaten on patios, balconies, or outdoor living areas, nor shall dust, rubbish or litter be shaken, swept or thrown from any window, door patio, balcony or outdoor living area. No laundry shall be aired from any balcony, or any other common area.

(c) No bicycles, toys, barbecue sets, tires, tools, ladders, or any other items shall be stored or left on any limited common areas which are stored or left in an unsightly manner, subject to such regulations as the Council may from time to time issue.

V. Noise

No unit owner or occupant shall play or be allowed to play any musical instrument, radio, television, phonograph, sound movie projector, tape recorder or like device, or shall practice singing or vocal exercises; or shall use any tool or engage in any noisy activity, if the same shall reasonably disturb and annoy the owners or occupants of any other unit. No unit owner shall engage in any altercation at any time or otherwise shout, yell, or disturb the peace if the same shall reasonably annoy and disturb the owners or occupants of any other unit. Television, radio and other electrical devices subject to volume control shall not be played above moderate levels if any unit owner or occupant objects, regardless of time of day.

VI. Cleanliness

All unit owners and occupants shall be responsible for the cleanliness of their respective units and appurtenant limited common elements. The cost of exterminating any rodent or insect infestation resulting from the uncleanliness of any unit shall be charged to the owner of that unit.

VII. Equipment and Installations

No unit owner or occupant shall tamper or interfere with, attempt to repair, alter, or make a connection with, any electrical or other cable, line, pipe, apparatus, or equipment without obtaining the written consent of Council. Similarly, before installing and operating any machinery, refrigerating or heating device, washing machine, dryer, air conditioning or other equipment not installed by the Developer-Builder, and before using any illumination other than electric light or decorative candles, each unit owner and occupant intending to install or operate same shall in each and every instance obtain the written consent of Council, which shall be promptly given or denied on considerations of safety.

VIII. Explosives and Inflammables

No explosive or highly inflammable material shall be brought into any portion of the condominium project, except under the supervision of the Council.

IX. Owner/Developer's Privileges

To the extent reasonably necessary or convenient for completion of construction of the condominium project, and sale or rental of units standing in the Owner/Developer's name, the Owner/Developer, its successors and assigns shall not be bound to observe the foregoing Rules.

The undersigned acknowledge the receipt of the accompanying Rules of Conduct for _____ dated November 2, 19____. It is understood that said Rules have been promulgated by the Condominium Council pursuant to its powers under the Code of Regulations, and that the Rules govern the conduct of the undersigned and all other residents of

NAME _____   UNIT NUMBER _____

DATE _____

7-13   LETTER REQUESTING CORRECTION OF A VIOLATED RULE

Dear _____:

As managing agent of the _____ Condominiums, we have recently made an inspection of the site. It was noted at that time that the window dressings in your home do not comply with the regulations in the Rules of Conduct. A copy of the section of the Rules of Conduct that is applicable is hereby enclosed.

Please arrange to have these window dressings removed within 15 days.

We appreciate the co-operation we have always received from the homeowners in _____ Condominiums and look forward to a continued good relationship.

Very truly yours,

7-14 LETTER TO OWNER ON INFRACTION OF RULES

Dear _____:

      As a _____ homeowner, we know you share our concern for the appearance of our condominium project. At the monthly meeting of the Council, window coverings and landscaping were two of the main topics. It was decided that tenants would also be given copies of the additions to the Rules of Conduct. This is to advise you that a copy of the enclosed material will also be delivered to your tenant, with the exception of the statement of account.

      We are sure that you have already given your tenant a copy of the Rules of Conduct that you received. This should be a part of any lease drawn up between a _____ homeowner and a tenant. If, for some reason, your tenant did not receive a copy of the Rules of Conduct, please send him a copy.

      We would like to thank you for your co-operation. By working together we will keep _____ a pleasant place to live and enhance the value of our condominium.

                                  Sincerely,

7-15 "WELCOME" LETTER TO TENANT FROM PROPERTY MANAGER

Dear _____:

WELCOME TO THE _____ APART-
MENTS!

It is our sincere desire to make your residence a happy experience by providing efficient and courteous service at all times, and by exerting every effort to maintain a pleasant atmosphere in keeping with one of __(city)'s__ most beautiful apartment buildings.

If you have any requests for service, please call me at ___-_____ or ___-_____. As your Resident Manager, residing at Apartment 203, I will be happy to explain the operation of the heating and air conditioning systems and advise you on the hanging of pictures, mirrors and/or other fixtures.

All requests for repairs and maintenance must be made to me at the numbers listed above.

We are pleased that you have selected our _____ Apartments as your home and are looking forward to a long-lasting relationship with you!

Sincerely,

7-16   ADDENDUM TO LEASE—PLUS COVER LETTER

Dear ——————————:

Enclosed please find an addendum to your lease for your consideration.

Please sign both copies of the addendum, have your signatures witnessed and return both copies to this office by

————————.

If we have not received both copies of the addendum properly signed and witnessed by ——————————, we will understand that you do not wish to consider the addendum, and your lease will then be considered terminated. We will then expect possession of the premises and the keys in our office on or before

————————.

It is our hope that you will wish to remain with us for another year or more.

Sincerely yours,

ADDENDUM TO LEASE

Dated _____

Between _____ Company

and

_____

The parties expressly agree that the said lease is expressly modified in the following respects:

Term _____

Commencement Date: _____

Expiration Date: _____

Total Rental for Entire Term _____

Equal Monthly Installments: _____

Maximum Number of Occupants: _____
All other terms and conditions of said lease shall remain the same.
Tenant is to submit the following information:

Employed By: _____   _____
             Husband   Wife

Company Address: _____   _____

Telephone Number: _____   _____

Type & Make Car: _____ _____
A copy of the Landlord-Tenant Code Summary was provided
with the original.

_____ Company, Agents

_____

Witness   Company Signature

Witness   Tenant

Witness   Tenant

7-17 MODEL REMINDER FOR OVERDUE RENT

Dear _____:

REMINDER

This is a reminder that your rent in the amount of _____ was due on the _____ day of the month.

If this rent has been paid, please disregard this notice, if not, will you please call the office, ____ _____.

Sincerely,
PROPERTY MANAGEMENT DE-
PARTMENT

_____

_____, Bookkeeper

7-18 REMINDER ON RENT LATE CHARGE

Dear _____:

REMINDER

Thank you for your recent payment of your rent. Please note that it did not include the late charge of $_____.

Please remit payment of the above by return mail. Thank you.

Sincerely,
PROPERTY MANAGEMENT
DEPARTMENT

_____

_____, Bookkeeper

7-19 REQUESTING PAYMENT OF LATE RENT

Dear _____:

AMOUNT DUE $_____

In accordance with the Landlord-Tenant Code of the State of _____, you are hereby notified that your rent must be paid in full within Five (5) days from the receipt of this notice.

If the full amount of rent, plus all penalties due, is not paid within five (5) days from the receipt of this notice, we will be forced to bring court action.

Very truly yours,

_____ Company

7-20 MODEL LETTER PROMISING THAT MAINTENANCE WORK WILL BE COMPLETED

Dear _____:

Thank you for your letter regarding maintenance work that has not been completed. We regret the inconvenience you have been caused.

Your letter has been forwarded to the owner and to the maintenance man who was to have completed the work. If any of the work remains unfinished within one week from the receipt of this letter, please call our operator and advise her of this.

We appreciate having tenants who care about their homes and want to make every effort to correct the problems.

Very truly yours,

_____ Company

_____

Property Manager

7-21 LETTER-AGREEMENT AUTHORIZING AGENT TO LOCATE NEW TENANT

Dear _____:

AGREEMENT

We do hereby request the _____ Company to find a new tenant for the premises located at:

_____

It is our understanding that the charge for this service is $_____. Our check is enclosed for this amount.

We acknowledge that this charge is for locating a new tenant for our apartment, and does not release us from our lease. Upon execution of a lease between _____ Company and a new tenant, we understand that our lease will be terminated as of the date of the new lease.

_____

Witness

_____

Tenants

7-22 ACKNOWLEDGING TENANT'S PLANS TO VACATE

Dear _____:

Thank you for your letter advising that you wish to vacate the premises. In accordance with the terms of your lease you are responsible for the rent until _____ or until we have an executed lease by a new tenant. If you wish us to try to find a new tenant, please sign and return the enclosed agreement.

The property will be inspected before you vacate and again after it is vacant. If you wish to be present for either of these inspections, please call our office for an appointment. If we do not hear from you, we will use our key for the inspection.

One of the main causes for deductions from deposits is the condition of the appliances. We must charge $25.00 for cleaning the range, refrigerator & exhaust fan. Other cleaning will be charged accordingly. Removal of trash & other items left in the apartment or basement or outside the apartment building will also be deducted. It is our desire to refund to you your entire deposit.

Please notify us, in writing, of your exact vacating date and your forwarding address. Your security deposit will be processed within 30 days after the termination date of your lease. If we can be of any assistance, please call us.

Sincerely,

_____ Company

7-23 LETTER REQUESTING COMPANY CONFIRMATION OF TRANSFER

Thank you for your letter advising that you have been transferred and must terminate your lease. Please have your company confirm this transfer so that you can be released from your lease. Your notice is effective _____.

Sincerely,

7-24 NOTE REQUESTING TENANT TO CONTACT OFFICE

Dear _____:

We have been unable to reach you in order to set up appointments to show your apartment.

Please contact our office as soon as possible:___- _____ . Thank you.

Sincerely,

7-25 MODEL INSPECTION REQUEST

Dear _____:

    I would like to inspect your apartment on _____
_____. I hope this will be convenient for you.

    If you cannot be at home, please make arrangements to
leave your key with a neighbor.

    Thank you for your co-operation.

                      Sincerely,

7-26 TURNING DOWN APPLICATION

Dear _____:

    Thank you for the application you recently submitted for
an apartment at _____

    One of the other applications we received has been ac-
cepted. Your application was considered but could not be accepted
for the following reason: _____

    We are glad that you came to our company and hope that
we will be able to work with you sometime in the future.

                      Sincerely,

7-27 MODEL WARNING ON LATE PAYMENTS

Dear _____:

As a Rental Agent, our office is contacted frequently for a credit reference on our tenants.

Late payments can give you a bad credit record.

Please help us to keep your name off the delinquent list by having your payments in our office on time each month. Your payments should be mailed to the Property Management Department, since you cannot be credited with the payment until it has been received here.

Address your payments as follows:

_____ Company

1102 _____ Street

_____, _____

Attention: Property Management Department

Thank you for your co-operation.

Sincerely,

Chapter 8

How to Use Letters to Make More Sales to Real Estate Investors

The sale of investment real estate is an unemotional matter, a matter of facts and figures. These 17 model letters will help you deal with investing clients and present crucial information effectively . . .

8-1   BRIEF LETTER DESCRIBING NEW INVESTMENT PROPERTY LISTING

Dear _____:

    I have a very fine investment property located at _____. It is in good condition, has an excellent rental record, and is in one of the better rental areas of _____.

    The owner will sell it on a land contract basis for 20–50% down. I am enclosing an information sheet for your study.

    When you will have an opportunity to see this property, please give me a call.

                         Sincerely,

8-2 MODEL LETTER TO A COMPANY DESCRIBING A BUILDING SITE

Dear _____:

I met you when your office was at _____. I was visiting with Mr. _____ the other day and mentioned to him that I had a good land listing.

This listing consists of 2.58 acres of ground and is offered at a very competitive price—$1.87 a square foot. This might be a fine location for your company if you should wish to build. One advantage to building is that you can get exactly what you want. This property is located at _____, and is very accessible from all parts of the city. The access to the property from the street is excellent, also.

I will contact you early next week concerning this property, and we can discuss it further.

Sincerely,

8-3   LETTER TO A MOTEL INVESTOR

Dear _____:

It was nice visiting with you yesterday. In connection with our conversation I have two motels that are located in good areas and show a fine return. One is west of _____, and the other is east of _____.

There are many items that one should consider when investing in a motel. I will relate to you some pertinent considerations. You should know how much the existing establishment will cost. You should also know how much business it will realistically do. (This is determined by going over the gross receipts from room sales and from auxiliary operations—such as a bar and a restaurant. In the case of a motel, the paramount factor in producing business is the location.) Finally, it is important that you know what the anticipated return on your investment can be. This is measured by two things: (1) The estimated costs of operating the motel at different percentage levels of capacity. By subtracting these costs from the gross revenues you will see the projected return on the total investment (both equity and debt); (2) The important relationship between equity and debt. The higher the equity you have the greater the leverage. In this same connection, the higher the debt the greater the return (or loss) to you.

When you plan to come to our town, please let me know and I will arrange to show both of these outstanding investments to you.

Sincerely yours,

KIRBY YOWELL
REALTORS

9312-14 BINNEY, OMAHA, NEBRASKA 68134, (402) 572-7770

ESTIMATED PROJECTION WORKSHEET

ADDRESS:
TYPE: Apartment Complex
DATE:

THE FOLLOWING EXAMPLE IS BASED ON __1ST__ YEAR ANNUAL FIGURES

1					EST. ALLOC. TO LAND	30,525		11.1%	1
2					EST. ALLOC. TO BLDG.	244,475		88.9%	2
3					EST. ALLOC. TO PERS. PROP.				3
4					TOTAL COST	275,000			4

	LOANS	Monthly Payment	Annual Payment	Int Rate	Annual Interest	Annual Principal	Yrs.	LOANS	AMOUNT		
5	1st.	1911	22,932	8 %	16,000	6,932	15	1st.	200,000		5
6	2nd.			%				2nd.			6
7	3rd.			%				3rd.			7
8	Chattel			%				Chattel			8
9	TOTALS							TOTAL LOANS	200,000		9
10		"A"	"B"	"C"	"D"	"E"		EQUITY	75,000		10

IMPORTANT!

The information on this "Estimated Projection Worksheet" is intended as an EXAMPLE ONLY, to demonstrate estimated spendable income, percentage returns and possible income tax consequences. All figures and percentages shown on this worksheet are estimates only! All information, allocations and projections shown on this worksheet, while based upon information supplied by the owner or from other sources deemed to be reliable, are not in any way warranted by Bohman Company. Independent tax counsel should be obtained concerning all income tax considerations involved.

Copyright © 1965 by DUNCAN, KORB & TRIMBLE, INC., REALTORS

Gross Rents	43,920			11
Other Income	480			12
SCHEDULED GROSS INCOME		44,400		13
ANNUAL EXPENSES:	Prop. Taxes	6,913.86		14
	Insurance	936.00		15
Heat & Water	2,300			16
Supplies	400			17
Management	1,980			18
Maint.	540			19
Misc.	400			20
TOTAL EXPENSES		13,469.88		21
(Before Loan Payments) NET INCOME		30,930.14		22
(Line 9-D) TOTAL INTEREST	16,000			23
(Line 9-E) TOTAL PRINCIPAL	6,932			24
TOTAL LOAN PAYMENTS		22,932		25
CASH FLOW		7,998.14		26

27	BASED ON EQUITY OF $ 75,000 (Line 10)	(The Cash Flow (Line 26) & "%" Return	7,998	or 10.7 %	27
28		(The "Equity Increase" (Line 24) & "%" Return	6,932	or 9.2 %	28
29		**THIS YEAR'S TOTAL RETURN**		or 19.9 %	29

30		(Line 13) GROSS INCOME	44,400	30
31	INCOME TAX DEDUCTIONS:	(Line 21) TOTAL EXPENSES	13,469.86	31
32		(Line 23) TOTAL INTEREST	16,000	32
33	(Method: 40 yrs - 1.25 dec. bal) BLDG. DEPRECIATION		7,640	33
34	(Method:) PERS. PROP. DEPREC.			34
35		**TOTAL DEDUCTIONS**	37,110	35
36		**THIS YEAR'S TAXABLE INCOME OR (TAX LOSS)**	7,290	36

SUMMARY "A" WHERE (TAX LOSS) IS SHOWN ON LINE 36				**SUMMARY "B"** WHERE TAXABLE INCOME IS SHOWN ON LINE 36		
37	(Line 29) THIS YEAR'S TOTAL RETURN		(Line 29) THIS YEAR'S TOTAL RETURN	7,290	37
38	EST. TAX SAVINGS (Tax Bracket × Line 36)		30% Bracket Est. Tax Payable on Taxable Income (Tax Bracket x Line 36)	2,187	38
39	THIS YEAR'S TOTAL GAIN (Incl. Tax Savings)		THIS YEAR'S GAIN AFTER INCOME TAXES	5,103	39

PRINTED
IN U.S.A.

THIS YEAR'S SPENDABLE CASH......$ _____
(Line 26 + Line 38)

THIS YEAR'S SPENDABLE CASH......$ 5,811.14
(Line 26 − Line 38)

8-4 COVER NOTE AND ESTIMATED PROJECTION WORKSHEET

Dear _____:

I am enclosing an estimate projection worksheet which bases a return on investment on factors other than just a cash purchase.

This is an excellent unit and I feel it would provide you a good investment.

Sincerely,

8-5 LETTER TO A MOTEL CHAIN ON BUILDING SITE

Dear _____:

I was visiting with Mr. _____ last week concerning your company possibly building an Inn in our city.

Mr. _____ mentioned that he had discussed some locations with you and that you expressed an interest in the one along the Interstate near Main Street. I am enclosing the information I have obtained from Investment Properties, Inc. concerning this property.

When your schedule permits you to come to town, please advise me and I will show you these choice sights for a motel.

Sincerely,

8-6 PROPERTY DESCRIPTION TO BUILDER

Dear _____:

I talked to you last week concerning two lots, _____ and _____, and _____ and _____. I was glad to hear from you what builders will pay for lots in this location. This gives me a better idea of how to approach prospective purchasers.

I learned Friday that the one large lot that we have listed on _____ Avenue can possibly be split into two lots. The list price for both lots is $5,000. These are two nice level lots and I think you would find them excellent building lots. They also fall into your price range.

Please study these offerings and I will call you toward the end of the week.

Sincerely,

8-7   CONCISE DESCRIPTION OF INVESTMENT PROPERTIES

Dear _____:

Enclosed are the three answers you asked for during our telephone conversation.

1. Maenner Lot
   Size 132' × 115'
   Address _____ North _____ St.
   Price $37,000.00
2. The distance from the north side of _____ to the south boundary of _____ is approximately 355.5'.
3. Plat of area—see attached.

I am enclosing our sheet on a fine duplex. This is directly across the street from the 6-plex I showed you. This is a good investment. As I mentioned to you earlier, the 6-plex did sell—this neighborhood has come back to life.

I have found from experience, both personally and with clients, that it is smart to invest in properties that are approximately 10 years old. There are two basic reasons for this: (1) You can usually obtain a better purchase. (2) The rental ratio to vacancy is much better because this age unit does not have the costly frills. Sauna baths, etc. are nice, but are not necessary to the average tenant.

Thank you for your past confidence. When it is convenient with you, let's discuss these properties.

Sincerely,

8-8 GETTING A PROFESSIONAL INTERESTED IN A COMMERCIAL PROPERTY

Dear _____:

I was sorry that I could not interest my prospect in your home, but I do want to thank you for the opportunity to see it.

While we were visiting your home, Doctor, you mentioned that you might be interested in purchasing some commercial property. I would certainly like to visit you concerning this. Whenever it is convenient for you, please give me a call and we will discuss this matter. I have three choice locations I think would interest you.

Sincerely,

8-9 PROMOTING AN OFFICE CONDOMINIUM

Dear _____:

Have you considered the possibility of owning your own office? At _____ Square Professional Office Condominiums, you can become your own landlord, without assuming the headaches of management. You pay yourself the rent.

As an investment, _____ Square offers an excellent way to shelter income from heavy taxation. When compared to many other ventures, _____ Square stands as a very sound, low-risk investment. The enclosed brochure will give you an idea about this area's finest professional/executive office condominium project.

Better yet, I will be happy to make an appointment with you to discuss the benefits of ownership in _____ Square. In just 10 minutes, I can show you a computer-calculated printout of the substantial financial benefits that could accrue to you over a ten-year period at _____ Square. Construction of Phase I is completed, and Phase II will be ready this spring.

If you have an office space requirement, or if you are interested in the investment possibilities, just give me a call at _____. We'll appreciate, too, your mentioning _____ Square to your friends and business associates.

Sincerely,

8-10 ATTEMPTING TO LIST A COMMERCIAL PROPERTY

Dear _____:

It has come to my attention that you own the following described property.

_____

Your brother, who is a close friend of mine, mentioned that you are interested in selling the property. If this is so, I would certainly like to talk to you about this matter. I have tried to call you several times, but I have been unsuccessful in my attempts. I work with many investors and I am confident that I could successfully sell your property.

I am enclosing my business card, and I would appreciate a call from you when it is convenient. When you call, I can obtain from you the necessary facts that will permit me to work-up a Broker's Reconstruction Form. This form will help us arrive at a marketable price on your property since it takes all costs and income into consideration.

Please call me as soon as you have the time.

Sincerely yours,

8-11   MODEL EXPLANATION OF RATE OF RETURN

Dear _____ :

     Enclosed are the answers to the questions that were brought up concerning the property located at _____ .

     1. What are the comparable rentals in the area?

_____ Apartments 48th-49th Street, _____ to _____ and

          48th-49th Street, _____ to _____

1 bedroom—$100-$215 per month unfurnished
2 bedroom—$130-$165 per month unfurnished
_____ Brothers _____
1 bedroom—$90.00 per month unfurnished
2 bedroom—$135.00 per month unfurnished

     According to this, this 6-plex is very much in the ball park as far as rentals. Both Mr. _____ and Mr. _____ expressed the same sentiment I mentioned, the rental demand in this area is fantastic.

     2. What is the rate of return? The rate of return is approximately 11.37%. I arrived at this by the most common formula used. The formula is as follows:

Vacancy, 5% of gross rental	$ 483.00
Maintenance, 5% of gross rental	483.00
Taxes	1,769.00
Heat, light and gas	548.00
Insurance	239.00
	$3,522.00

     I took the expenses and subtracted them from the gross rental. Then I divided by the purchase cost. This shows the approximate 11.37% return.

     3. How many furnaces and air conditioners? There are 6 of each.

4. Who owns the parking lot east of the 6-plex? It is a restricted parking area that is leased by the apartment owners on _____ and _____.

5. Why is one 2-bedroom apartment rented for $175.00 per month while the other three are rented for $135.00 per month? The $175.00 per month apartment is furnished. I talked to Mrs. _____ this morning and she told me this apartment was rented yesterday noon for $180.00. Thus the gross income should be $9,660.00 instead of $9,600.00.

6. Is the present loan assumable, and if so, would there be an interest charge? I talked to Mr. _____ at _____ Savings this morning and he told me that the loan is assumable with an interest charge. The interest would be approximately 7½ to 7¾%.

If you have any further questions, please call. I feel that this 6-plex would be an excellent investment for you. I am convinced that it is one of the best 6-plexes for the money in _____. After calling and visiting with Mr. _____, owner of _____ Brothers Realty, and the owner of an apartment complex nearby, I am convinced this area has turned the corner and is beginning to appreciate in value. Mr. _____ said he has had good occupancy, and the demand is consistent. A new super-discount store and bank are moving into this area. I also have a client who is seriously considering investing in a large commercial tract at approximately _____. We have seen a movement of many folks from the suburbs back to the center of the city.

Mr. _____, I am convinced that this would be a sound investment at $50,000.00.

Sincerely,

8-12 MODEL LETTER PRESENTING DATA ON INVESTMENT PROPERTY

Dear _____:

Concerning the 11-unit apartment we inspected, the payment is $1,050.60 per month. This includes the principal, interest and taxes. The original length of the mortgage was 20 years and there are approximately 19 years remaining.

The unit breakdown is as follows:

No	Rent	
1	$217.00	1 garage
2	150.00	
3	130.00	
4	165.00	
5	125.00	
6	140.00	1 garage
7	70.00	
8	160.00	1 garage
9	130.00	
10	135.00	
11	140.00	1 garage

Listed below are other important data:

INVESTMENT PROPERTY—FACTORS TO FIGURE

5% Vacancy	$937.20
5% Maintenance	But if you are doing the work, the expense would be approximately $300.00; Snow removal and supplies.
Taxes	$3,048.32
Heat	540.00
Insurance	400.00
	$5,061.30

Costs from gross divided by purchase price = return
Gross $18,744.00 + $300.00 for washer & dryer per
                   300.00   year, not the $450.00
                $19,044.00

The return shows approximately 11.46%

There is one washer and one dryer. Mr. _____
changed to a coin operated washer. The annual income from these
is approximately $300.00.

                                        Sincerely,

8-13 PROMOTING SENIOR CITIZEN FULL-CARE CENTER AS AN INVESTMENT

Dear _____:

It was nice talking with you last Friday concerning the possibility of your company investing in a total care facility for senior citizens. This would be ideal if it could be worked in the new medical complex.

This type of care facility is badly needed in this city. It came to my mind while I was visiting with my in-laws, who are looking for such a facility. I called _____ and mentioned this to him. He said that there is ground available near

_____

I certainly feel that a project of this nature is worth pursuing. A care unit of this nature would be good for the whole community. There is a hidden demand for a total care facility.

If your company would like to investigate this matter, I would be glad to visit with you. Just give me a call.

Sincerely,

8-14 LETTER SEEKING INVESTOR REFERRALS

Dear _____:

When your clients decide to sell their home and/or their business in order to move to either _____ or _____, all in sunny _____, why not refer them to us at _____ Realty?

We handle all types of real property, home purchase or leasing, business opportunities, commercial investments and land. Anyone sent to us will receive our V.I.P. treatment. We will supply them with maps, literature describing local places of interest, as well as meet them at the airport . . . all directed to make their move smooth, rapid and pleasant.

Any referrals resulting in a completed purchase, signed, sealed and delivered will earn your organization a 20% referral fee. We, in turn, would direct referrals to your attention for anyone moving to your area. Would you please take the time to advise us of your interest?

We look forward to a long and lasting association with your organization which will be beneficial to both of us.

Very truly yours,

8-15 LETTER TO ANOTHER AGENT ON BEHALF OF AN INVESTOR

Dear _____:

I talked to my client about the property on Highway __, and he said the building is too small.

He needs 10,000–12,000 square feet of land and must have a building with at least 4,000 square feet on one level. He can construct the building. He also needs to be by an active store such as the _____ grocery store.

If you should discover something like this, I would certainly appreciate hearing from you.

Sincerely,

8-16 SEEKING AVERAGE OFFICE SPACE COST FIGURES

Dear _____:

On the advice of Mr. _____, _____ Real Estate Board Executive, I am writing you to obtain some information concerning the cost per square foot of office space in principal cities throughout the United States.

The organization I am writing for is thinking of opening offices in many major cities such as—New York, Chicago, Houston, Boston, and San Francisco. They would need about 1,000 square feet per office.

If you have an average cost figure, I would certainly appreciate hearing from you. Thank you.

Sincerely,

8-17   COVERING LETTER FOR BROKER'S RECONSTRUCTION PROPERTY ANALYSIS FORM*

Dear _____:

Enclosed is the Broker's Reconstruction Property Analysis Form. This is the form that we talked about last night in our telephone conversation. No analysis is perfect, but this type has proven to be correct in the vast majority of cases.

Being the knowledgeable investor that you are, I am sure that after studying this form you will agree that the purchaser's offer of $42,500 is very close.

I am serving you as a counsellor, and in this capacity I would certainly recommend that you accept this offer. We have showed your property approximately 15 times, and this is the first offer. You have until Friday to let me know your decision.

Thank you for your continued confidence in our firm.

Sincerely,

---

*Note: Form B of the Realtors National Marketing Institute is an excellent form for determining the value of investment property. This form can be obtained from the Realtors National Marketing Institute in Chicago, Illinois. Form B cannot be reproduced other than in the Realtors National Marketing Institute's publications.

Chapter 9

Effective Publicity
and Public Relations
Letters

Continuous promotion of your company and of the individuals in it is one of the keys to consistent success in the real estate business. The following twenty-four model letters will make it easy for you to keep your company and your accomplishments before the public. . . .

9-1 "I'VE DONE IT AGAIN!!"—MODEL LETTER AFTER SUCCESSFUL SALE

Dear _____:

I've done it again! I sold the house at _____!

Your new neighbors, _____, will be moving in shortly. Won't you please welcome them to your lovely neighborhood?

Through the sale of this home, I have several other clients interested in locating in this area. If you know of anyone that might be interested in selling, I'd appreciate a call.

If, at any time I can be of service to you in any real estate need, either buying or selling, I hope you will call on me.

Sincerely,

9-2 PROMOTING A LAND LISTING

Dear _____:

　　　　We believe you'll be interested in this information about the southwest corner of _____.

Size: 348,480 square feet, more or less (8 acres).

Price: $300,000 ($.86 per square foot).

Zoning: R-9 except for a 60-foot strip on P-1 on north, south, and east sides.

Subdivision into Office-Building Lots: This is a definite possibility. We have a layout showing how this could be done, plus estimated income/expense and investor profit.

　　　　The potential to an investor or investor group is favorable. Please call me if you'd like to see the layout and dollar figures.

Commission: For the sale of the property, we'll pay your firm 75% of the 6% commission. I'll be glad to assist in every way possible. Just give me a call.

　　　　　　　　　　　　　　　　　　Sincerely,

9-3 PROMOTING COMMERCIAL/INVESTMENT DIVISION

Dear _____:

As any forward-looking organization must do in today's fast changing world, _____ Realtors once again are keeping pace in order to serve our clients in a broader range and more professionally.

We will continue to give expert service in residential sales, homeowner's and auto insurance, and appraising. We have kept abreast in these areas by completing our *Certified Residential Broker's* (C.R.B.) Designation—a designation given by the National Institute of Real Estate Brokers for residential brokers—by associating ourselves with a top-rated insurance company and by receiving appraisal licenses from the _____ Real Estate Commission.

We have embarked upon a new and rewarding field for many of our clients, the field of *Commercial and Investment Real Estate*. As everyone knows, real estate has been the best investment for people throughout the years. This is primarily so because it offers investors many advantages—tax shelter, liquidity, low risk factor, appreciation, leverage and expert management if one does not wish to manage his own investment properties.

We recommend that you have other investments as well, but real estate should be included in everyone's program.

Whenever it would be convenient for you to visit with us about this area of investment, please feel free to call.

Your friends,

9-4 SHOPPING AND OFFICE PARK PROMOTION

Dear _____:

On Wednesday, October 18, I had the privilege of being invited to an hour-long seminar on the _____ Development. This is the new office park and shopping center that is being constructed by the _____ Development Company at _____ Ave. and _____ West St.

The reason for this short letter is to ask you to remember me if you might know of some company that would be interested in buying or leasing space in this fine location.

The agent for this addition is the _____, Co. They are cooperating with all Realtors in this endeavor.

If you know of someone who might be interested, please ask them to get in touch with me.

Cordially,

9-5   SEEKING LISTINGS—A PROMOTIONAL APPROACH

Dear _____:

   We are equipped to offer our services in all areas of
_____, but to be more knowledgeable and to offer
superior and professional real estate service, we are mainly going to
concentrate in the following areas:

   1. _____ Country Club
   2. West _____
   3. _____ Suburban
   4. Southwest _____
   5. _____ Fairmont

   We know these areas well and have had a very successful
record in them. Here are some of our recent sales:

4466 _____   8320 _____Dr.

4921 _____   1513 _____Dr.

8114 _____   1421 _____Dr.

6636 _____   _____ So. 117th

_____ No. 78th   836 No. _____

_____ So. 121st   7743 _____

_____ No. 55th   5503 _____

1509 _____Dr.   8753 _____

1502 _____Dr.   9733 _____

9406 _____   3105 _____Rd.

1214 _____   _____ No. 107th Ave.

10265 _____Dr.   7802 _____Dr.

10503 _____Rd.   _____ No. 14th

7738 _____   6620 _____

_____ No. 50th Ave.   1816 W. _____

_____ No. 17th   _____ No. 61st

5649 _____   _____ No. 47th Ave.

5143 _____   8505 _____

     Thank you for reading this letter and please remember our young, vigorous, sales-oriented organization.

     WE WOULD CERTAINLY LIKE THE OPPORTUNITY OF VISITING WITH YOU CONCERNING OUR POSITIVE APPROACH TO SELLING HOUSES BEFORE YOU GIVE ANYONE ELSE THE AUTHORIZATION TO SELL.

                                          Serviceably yours,

9-6 PROMOTING A UNIQUE HOME DEVELOPMENT

Dear _____:

_____ Ranch consists of about 160 acres located in the mountains about twenty miles south of _____, _____. It's an old homestead that is now surrounded by the _____ National Forest and is readily accessible via a good gravel Forest Service road.

The Ranch has been planned to serve as a private ranch for between six and eight families. The concept is to provide for each of its owners everything that he would have if he were to go out and buy his own ranch, but at less cost and with far less time and trouble.

You can become an owner by purchasing a homesite of four or more acres plus an undivided interest in much of the property including most of the meadowlands and creeks.

At the present time, the ranch is staffed and operating. We have two corrals, twenty or so horses, lots of tack, all necessary maintenance equipment, a large arena and even a few steers and calves for roping. The two creeks that run through the property are most fishable.

Our company, which is responsible for putting this concept into being, will have a representative there at all times to make things as easy and convenient as possible for an owner. We can act as builders after a site has been purchased; we can supply horses, and care for your horses; plow your driveway; clean your house; shovel the snow off your roof; provide pack trips and hunter outfitting—or just about anything else you might want or need. Equally important, if you want to do it all yourself, we're even willing to leave you alone!

My family and I live in a log house on one of the sites at the ranch. The foreman _____ _____, his wife, and son live on another. At the present time, we are seeking to sell five additional homesites. These locations are beautiful and each has an excellent panoramic view of the rugged _____ Mountain landscape. They are not inexpensive. The sites vary somewhat in price, but average about fifty thousand dollars each. In addition, each owner will purchase his share of about sixty acres of grazing and fishing land.

We believe that _____ Ranch is unique; not only in its concept but in its proximity to _____. Here, when one so desires, one can ski on _____ Mountain (the largest vertical drop in America), play tennis, golf on a championship course, attend rodeos, shoot the white water on the _____, or participate in a myriad of other activities available in this resort area. Equally important, one can take a horse from the ranch and ride in the mountains day after day without ever seeing anyone.

If _____ Ranch sounds like something that might interest you, I suggest that you contact your real estate broker. If you don't have one, you may feel free to call on me by phone or by mail for further information. _____ of the _____ Agency in _____ is our broker and will also welcome any inquiries—particularly if you happen to be in the _____ area.

For your interest, we have enclosed some maps and pictures to help give you an idea of where and what _____ Ranch is.

Sincerely,

9-7 "MEET YOUR NEW NEIGHBOR"

Dear _____:

     May we introduce your new neighbors? They are Mr. & Mrs. _____, who have purchased the home at _____.

     In promoting the sale of this property, we talked with other potential buyers who are interested in your neighborhood, but we did not have listings that would fill their requirements.

     If you for any reason desire to sell your property, we will be glad to give you up-to-date information on market possibilities.

                           Sincerely,

9-8 LISTING FARM PROMOTION

Dear _____:

About a week ago, you probably received a letter from my broker saying that I wished to specialize in your neighborhood. This letter is to confirm that fact, and to let you know that if you have any questions regarding real estate, I'll be glad to talk to you.

Enclosed is some information regarding the new "Real Estate Settlement Procedure Act." It is important that you be aware of this law, because it may directly affect any future purchase or sale of your home.

As part of a service to you and your neighbors, I'd like to keep you posted on laws such as this that directly relate to buyers and sellers of real estate.

Sincerely,

9-9 KEEPING IN TOUCH WITH CLIENTS

Dear _____:

Recently I talked to you on the telephone regarding real estate. As I mentioned then, we have been of service to you in the past, either as the listing or selling agent of your house.

If you were satisfied with our work, please call me if you ever have need for a real estate agent again. I'd also appreciate it if you could refer my name to your friends and acquaintances.

Looking back over economic conditions of the past few years, now is the best time to sell or buy a house. Interest rates are down from last year and money is readily available.

I'll be glad to discuss real estate with you—and remember, I will give you a free appraisal upon request.

Sincerely,

9-10   THE "POSITIVE APPROACH" TO CLIENTS

Dear _____:

There has been an exciting change in my life and I want you to be one of the first to know of it! I am now listing and selling real estate properties for _____, Realtors.

The main reason for my excitement is that _____, Realtors, the POSITIVE APPROACH Realtors, has a proven record of success through honest and reliable service to their customers in listing and selling homes. Their Comprehensive Marketing Plan is designed to SELL properties. As members of Multiple Listing Service, Local and National Real Estate Associations, and National Referral Programs, you, the customer, are guaranteed service second to none.

Because we belong to the Multiple Listing Service, we and approximately 600 other salespeople are actively working for you. This also allows me to show and sell any home listed with any other firm, not only those listed with us.

SO . . . please let me explain this POSITIVE APPROACH at no obligation to you. REMEMBER . . . in professional selling these three points have always been and will continue to be the key:

1. IT'S NOT THE COMPANY ALONE. No company name alone sells homes.
2. It's the Company's PHILOSOPHY OF SERVICE.
3. And the INDIVIDUAL within that company that is serving you.

PLEASE . . . before you authorize any firm to sell your property, allow me to explain fully to you our POSITIVE APPROACH.

When you and any of your friends are interested in selling or buying a home, please allow me to assist you.

Thank you.

Sincerely,

9-11 COMPANY'S ACCOMPLISHMENTS TO NEW SALES ASSOCIATES

Dear _____:

WELCOME TO REAL ESTATE AS A PROFESSION!

Every year thousands of people of every description think about going into Real Estate as a profession. This letter is intended to offer some valuable information on how to be successful in this most rewarding of careers. You will receive financial rewards and personal satisfaction

Sometimes a bright future has been doomed because a person chose the wrong organization. We feel _____ Realtors is the right company for you.

If you are looking for a future in real estate and not just a hobby, the following survey can help you. If the company you are thinking of can answer these questions "yes," you will have picked the right company.

1. Does the company name and reputation reflect integrity, dignity and success?
2. Does the company have a complete written policy book that you may review and discuss?
3. Will you actually be trained to help you succeed?
4. Does the company encourage full time association for maximum earnings?
5. Is the company planning expansion for greater opportunities for advancement?
6. Does the company have a Guaranteed Trade-In Program?
7. Can the company show a record of Realtor leadership?
   a. Star Salesman-Sales Executive Club _____ 19__
   b. Realtor of the Year _____ Suburban Board of Realtors
   c. President of _____ Suburban Multiple Listing Service

      d. President of _____ Suburban Board of Real-
         tors
      e. President of _____ Chamber of Commerce
      f. District Vice-President, _____ Association of
         Realtors
      g. Chairman Speakers Bureau, _____ Associa-
         tion of Realtors
      h. President, Associate Division, _____ Subur-
         ban Board of Realtors
      i. President _____ Holy Name Society
      j. Evergreen Park Representative _____
         _____ Council
      k. Treasurer for Sierra Club of_____ Suburban
         area
      l. Past President of Toastmaster Club

8. Is the broker an active Realtor and a leading member of Multiple Listing Service?
9. Does the company offer group hospitalization and life insurance?
10. Are offices open 7 days a week plus 5 evenings?
11. Does company have a planned advertising campaign?
12. Is the company located primarily in the area where you live and are active in community organizations?
13. Does the company have a fair compensation plan?

     At _____ Realtors we answer "yes" to all these important questions. You are invited to visit our offices and attend our training sessions.

                              Sincerely,

9-12 PROMOTING INSURANCE PLANS

Dear _____:

I certainly hope this note finds you and your family happy in the home that we were privileged in assisting you find. This note is to remind you that we have another very important service for you. We have a complete insurance program to offer our customers, with particular attention being placed on the following coverages: *Homeowners, Mortgage Redemption* and *Monthly Disability* coverage. We feel these coverages are very important to home ownership. If you would like us to explain these or any other coverages, please feel free to call us any time. We are associated with two fine organizations that assist us in this service. Thank you.

Sincerely yours,

9-13   "ANNUAL REPORT" IS GOOD

Dear _____:

Enclosed is our third annual _____ County real estate report. Even though there was a 5½% decrease in the deed transfers this past year over 19__, our production was up 46%. We made 257 sales for a total volume of just over 9 million dollars.

The average residential selling price from our office was $36,339. The percentage of our listings sold in 19__ was 82%.

Also enclosed is the 19__ Multiple Listing rankings from the _____ Board of Realtors. Although participating in MLS is not mandatory, and this represents only a third of our sales, we were pleased to be number one in this area of sales.

For your employees we have developed a marketing program to assist in their real estate needs. For incoming transferees, we have a "Welcome to _____" kit. For those moving out of _____, we have a national relocation service.

If we can be of service to your organization at any time, please feel free to call us.

Yours truly,

9-14   THANKS TO SPEAKER

Dear _____:

Thank you so much for taking time out of your busy schedule to address our Board. The weather was cold and blustery, thus curtailing our normal attendance, but those who were there certainly enjoyed your talk.

It is with deep appreciation that our association thanks you for taking part in our meeting.

Sincerely,

9-15   A PROBLEM IS SOLVED

Dear _____:

I was very sorry that the waterproofing man did not complete his job before your transaction closed. We were under the impression that the work had been completed. It was obviously lack of communication. "To err is human, to forgive divine," and we thank you so much for your gracious letter. Needless to say, we are pleased that your problem has been handled and we are sorry about any inconvenience.

Again, your kind words are much appreciated.

Sincerely,

9-16   A TAX INFORMATION NOTE TO CLIENT

Dear _____.

Please let me take this opportunity to thank you for buying from us this year.

It was a pleasure to be of service to you in this important decision. We certainly hope that you are happy with your purchase and that you will call on us if there is anything further we can do.

Be sure to make your return for tax purposes at the new _____ Building between January 1 and March 31. Do not forget to claim your homestead exemption at the county tax office. If you live in the city you will also have to make a city return. If I may help you by going with you to make your return, please feel free to call on me.

Please accept our best wishes for a Merry Christmas and a Happy and Prosperous New Year.

Sincerely yours,

9-17 THANK YOU NOTE AFTER CLOSING

Dear _____:

On the closing or "consummation" of your sale of _____, we have our third occasion to thank you for your confidence in our real estate services. As we indicated to you in a letter which followed your second transaction with us, repeat business implies a compliment. Most assuredly, this is true the third time around.

Be certain we shall try to merit your continued confidence in us.

Sincerely yours,

9-18 A THANK-U-GRAM

THANK-U-GRAM
A Message of Appreciation to You
A Grateful Acknowledgment to You
In recognition of the good you have done

Dear _____:

I want to thank you for your confidence in me during the purchase of your new home. Without people like you there would be no reason for me.

Thank you again, and when I can help you or your friends in the future, please call me.

Sincerely,

9-19   OFFERING SERVICES TO NEWLYWEDS

Dear _____:

Congratulations on your recent marriage—may the two of you have a lifetime of wonderful memories. We wish both of you continued success and good health.

I would sincerely appreciate your calling me anytime you or anyone you know may be interested in buying, selling or trading real estate. Of course, there is never an obligation.

Very truly yours,

9-20   THANKS TO NEWSPAPER EDITOR

Dear _____:

Mr. _____ and I both wish to thank you very much for your excellent article in the Real Estate section of Sunday's paper concerning our merger.

When I sent you the information I made one error. If you would please correct it for next week, we would certainly appreciate it. Mr. _____ has been in the real estate profession since 19__ and I have been in the profession since 19__, but we have not had our separate companies since that time. I began mine in April of 19__ and Mr. _____ began his in March of 19__.

Thank you again very much.

Sincerely,

9-21 "WELCOME ABOARD!" TO A NEW REALTOR

Dear _____:

It is with a great deal of pleasure that I am able to inform you that the Board of Directors has accepted your application for REALTOR membership in the _____ Board of Realtors. Welcome aboard! If there are any questions whatsoever that you may have regarding membership, I hope you will call us. Our purpose is to serve YOU, as a member of the Board.

The term REALTOR has taken on a special meaning in the minds of the public and has a connotation of competency, fairness, and high integrity resulting from adherence to moral conduct in business relations, exercised within the guidelines of the REALTORS Code of Ethics. This is a valuable image because this is what the public is seeking today.

We would like to invite you to involve yourself in the activities of our organization. No association such as ours can be successful without the participation of each member. We hope that you will make it a regular practice to attend our Wednesday noon membership meetings, which we hold at_____'s Restaurant.

We invite you to call at our Board Office, meet our staff and make a tour of the office. We will look forward to working with you in the years ahead.

Sincerely,

9-22 THANK YOU NOTE TO CO-BROKER

Dear _____:

Thank you for assisting us in the sale of our listing at
_____ Ave.

It was our pleasure to do business with your firm. Please do not hesitate to call us any time about our listings. We look forward to doing business with you again in the future.

Sincerely,

9-23   THANKS TO FELLOW BROKER FOR REFERRAL

Dear _____:

Good Morning! Good Afternoon! Good Evening!
No matter what time of day it is, it is always a pleasure to receive a referral from your company.

It was our pleasure to do business with your referral and today we successfully closed the sale with them. The following is a statement of commission received by our office and we are happy to enclose your referral fee. Let's do it again!

Sales Price	39,000.00
Commission	2,739.99
Cross-Sale (_____ & Assoc.)	1,365.00
Commission to _____ Co.	1,365.00
10% Referral fee	136.50

Sincerely yours.

9-24   THANKS TO A NEWSPAPER FOR CONTINUED
COOPERATION

Dear _____:

Thank you for the good food and pleasant company we received February 18, 19__ when the _____ hosted the officers and directors of the _____ Board of Realtors.

I personally enjoyed visiting with you at the table as well as listening to your short talk. You obviously have pride in your newspaper, in the_____'s facilities, and in all the dedicated people who work for the _____ shows.

I do get around the country a little and one of the first things I do is buy a paper especially to see what other real estate companies are doing in the way of advertising. I am always hoping to find new ideas I can use in my own business back home. In examining other newspapers, I have come to the conclusion that the _____ is a good newspaper and that_____ is a great place to live and do business.

Since classified advertising is generally the biggest single expense item for most real estate companies, it is only natural that to be good, and yet do an effective job while remaining competitive, all owners of real estate businesses constantly scrutinize their advertising as to effectiveness as well as to cost. Sometimes the relations between newspaper people and real estate people become strained because each side overlooks the fact that both have problems and both take pride in their services.

Your luncheon helped to keep open the necessary communications we both need, and pointed out that we are really allies not adversaries. If we can both give the best of service and can both profit, we are both happy.

Thank you again,

Chapter 10

Model Letters That Present Real Estate Appraisal Information Effectively

The following 13 letters provide you with models you can follow to present appraisal information concisely, clearly and effectively . . .

10-1 MODEL LETTER REPORTING APPRAISAL OF AN APARTMENT COMPLEX

Dear _____:

As you requested, I have inspected Lot 97, _____ addition, _____ County, _____, _____, commonly known as _____ North Street, and called "_____ Apartments." The lot is 104×1397.8 and consists of 1 acre of land with a creek at the far West end of the lot. This property is zoned "R-7," permitting multi-family uses. It is located close to _____ Street, a high traffic street, with excellent access to all parts of _____. There is a _____ Bldg. on the next lot North which has sales and various other offices occupied (this land sold for $39,000.00 in 19__ and now has a finished brick one-story structure on the land). Across _____ Street there is a service station, a large _____ supermarket; and 1 block East on Maple there is a drug store, various other new one-story office buildings and a large branch of the _____ Bank.

The improvements are all new (completed September, 19__) and include a concrete block foundation and frame 3-story apartment building with a brown stucco finish, trimmed with stone arches around all windows and entrances which contain a total of 21,000 sq. ft. on 3 floors; which is divided into 24 units of apartments. Six of these units are two bedroom, which are 810 sq. ft., each fully carpeted with shag carpeting, each containing a tiled bath with shower over tub, kitchen with all formica cabinets and tops, Whirlpool dishwasher, stove, hood, disposal and re-frigerator. Eighteen units are one bedroom apartments of 780 sq. ft., each all completed and finished similar to the two bedroom units. Each unit has its own private entrance off an enclosed porch.

Other improvements include 20 garages, all with individual lighting inside and on the exterior; these are built in 2 rows, easily accessible from a concrete paved drive and parking areas that lead to _____ Street on the east. Attached to the garages on the east is a neatly finished laundry room 12 × 30 ft. which contains 2 washers and 2 dryers for tenant usage.

The area around the _____ Apartments has 70' of neatly kept grass in the front as well as some 35–45 ft. on the east side plus 11–16 ft. of sodded area on the south and west. Sidewalks to this building are more than ample width 4' to 5', where normally we find 2' to 3' of walks for apartments of this type.

In our opinion it is to be noted that the apartment building ground floor is only 24" below grade area, where in most cases we find the lower level units some 4' below grade. The area where the garage exists also has been raised to a higher grade than originally existed and all have a full concrete foundation and concrete floors (not asphalt which is normally the method used in today's construction).

Although these units are 3 years old, after inspection we found all interiors are immaculately kept and all improvements are in new and excellent condition. Presently 22 of the 24 units are leased to tenants without children or pets. All are fully air-conditioned with electric units.

Currently the rent schedule's are:

6-2 bedroom units @ $210.00 per month
10-1   "   " @ $195.00 per month
5-1   "   " @ $185.00 per month
3-1   "   " @ $175.00 per month

In our opinion, the present market value of the property is:

Land: _____ $39,000
Improvements: $309,263
Total: _____ $348,263

If you have any questions, please call me.

Sincerely,

10-2 APPRAISAL LETTER FOR ESTATE PURPOSES

Dear _____:

I have inspected the property located at _____ North 55th Street, _____, _____. To the best of my judgment a fair market price as of both June 14, 19___ and June 14, 19___ would be $38,000.00 I arrived at this figure by checking comparable sales of similar houses in this given location.

Sincerely,

10-3 REPORTING ON APPRAISAL OF SEVERAL PROPERTIES

Dear _____:

As per your request, I am enclosing what I feel to be the market value of your properties:

1. Personal: Mr. Donald _____ and/or Joyce _____, Husband and Wife
2. _____ Electric, Inc., and
3. _____ Electric, Inc. of _____

The appraisals are as follows:

1. Personal

   a. _____ _____ Street

   This property I feel has a very limited use for the open market, but for Mr. & Mrs. _____'s purpose it has a high value—the ability to extend to the building located at _____ _____ Street. The area encompasses approximately 3,000 sq. ft. If the _____ had to go and buy this land today in order to expand their other building, they would pay whatever the market would bear—the market value could be approximately $37,500.00. It is zoned 1st Industrial. Legal description of above property is: Section 21, Township 11, Range 10, Triangle East 112.00′ North 421.73′ South 51.75′ North 269.75′ T.L.4.

   b. _____ _____ Street

   This is an outstanding brick veneer home with approximately 2146 square feet on the first floor. There is approximately 1700 square feet of living area in the lower level. The home has a 3-car garage—double in appearance, but with one section being a tandem type. By checking comparables in this location as used by the Multiple Listing System of the _____ Real Estate Board, I feel the market value of this home would be approximately $45,000. The lot size is 143′ × 168′ and it has water, sewer, and gas. Legal description: Lot 7 of _____ _____.

c. _____ _____ Street
_____ _____ is a vacant lot that is 143′
× 165′ and it has water, sewer and gas. I feel that the market
value would be approximately $5,700.00. Legal descrip-
tion: Lot 9 of _____ Replat.

d. Lot located at approximately _____ and
_____ Streets.
This lot is vacant and is zoned R7. The size of the lot is
approximately 118′ × 481′. It has water, sewer, paving and
gas. I feel that the market value is approximately $26,000.
Legal   description: Lot   90,   _____
_____.

2. _____ _____ Electric Inc.

a. _____ _____ Street
This property is zoned 1st Industrial. The lot size is 85′ ×
185′ and it has a 10,000 sq. foot building on it. 8,800 sq. ft.
is warehouse and 1,200 square feet is office space. The
property is located in a fast growing area of _____. I feel
the market value is as follows:
    Land—I figure $.40 a square foot = $7,290.00
    Building—I feel that this building is worth $5.00 a square
foot = $50,000.
The total composite should be worth approximately
$56,290.00. The legal description of this property is: Lot
70, _____ Park.

b. _____ _____ Street
This property is zoned 1st Industrial. The lot size is approximately 95′ × 140′ and it has a 12,000 square ft. building
on it. Of the 12,000 square feet: 2,500 square is display
space; 1,200 square feet is office; and 8,300 square feet is
warehouse space. I feel the market value of this property is
as follows:
    Land—I feel it is worth $750.00 a front foot =
$63,750.00
    Building—I feel this building is worth $8.50 a square foot
= $102,000.00

Composite—$165,750 approximate value.

Legal description:

West 58.24', North 130', Irregular East 140', West 455', South 150', North 210', Tx lot 4, Section 23, TWP 15, Range 12.

c. The following properties encompass approximately 10 acres of land which is zoned 1st Industrial. I am basing my appraisal on land value which I feel is appropriate in this situation.

1. Lots 73, 74, 75 of _____—approximately 6.45 acres—Property has a farm house with a double garage, a barn and out-building. Utilities are water and gas.

2. _____ _____ Ave—Lot size is 109' × 175'.—Lot 11 _____ Park Replat—Small house with water and gas.

3. _____ _____ Ave.—Lot size is 109' × 175'—Lot 8 _____ Park Replat—vacant lot with water and gas.

These properties have approximately 7.33 acres of land. I feel the market value of this property is approximately $112,000.00

3. _____ Electric, Inc. of _____

44 _____ Road—220' North of _____ Road on _____ Street.

Legal description—North 100' of Lot 192, N. W. quarter of S. W. quarter Section 8, Township 10, North Range 7

Lot size is 100' × 149'. The zoning is H-2—Highway 2. Water, gas, paving and sewer are in and paid for. Checking with both the owner and other people familiar with _____ property, it looks like the market value should be approximately $16,000.00

If you have any questions, please contact me.

Sincerely,

10-4 APPRAISAL INFORMATION ON RESIDENTIAL PROPERTY

Dear _____:

Thank you for allowing us to appraise your lovely home. You had two very logical questions: (1) What is the market value of your property? (2) With this value what would be your approximate net if your property sells for this figure?

I will now answer your questions.

1. What is the market value of your property? I feel that your property should sell at approximately $35,000.00. It should be placed on the market at $35,950. I am enclosing a complete competitive market analysis to show you how I arrived at this figure.

2. With this value what would be your approximate net if your property sells for this figure? To answer this question I am enclosing an approximate net sheet.

Thank you again and whenever you are ready for our services, please call anytime. If you have any questions, please feel free to get in touch.

Sincerely yours,

(See attached material)

BALL REAL ESTATE
Locally Owned

KIRBY - YOWELL, REALTORS   OLD MILL CENTER

REAL ESTATE · MULTIPLE LISTING SERVICE · INSURANCE
626 North 108th Court.   Omaha, Nebraska. 68154   (402) 496-2000

COMPETITIVE MARKET ANALYSIS FORM

Date 11/4/76

COMPARABLES				SUBJECT PROPERTY		
1. ADDRESS	North 95th St.			Decatur St.		
1200	=	37,000	Sq. Ft.	1232	=	37,986.67
3			Bed Rm.	3		
1.75 + R/I			Baths	1.75 + R/I		
3001			Fam. Rm.	3001		
--			Rec. Rm.	--		
7 rooms			Carp/drapes	6 rooms	= -	100.00
			Fireplace	no	= -	1200.00
H/F, D/W, R/O, Disp			Kit App.	H/F, DW, R/O, Disp		
yes			A/C	yes		
2 car BI			Garage	2 car BI		
same			Lot	same		
better			Loc	good	-	2000.00
good			Cond.	good		
yes			Deck	yes		
no			Drapes	yes	+ 5(50)=	250.00
			TOTALS			$34,936.67

2. ADDRESS	1512 North	St.		Decatur		
1112	=	33,000	Sq. Ft.	1232	=	36,561.15
3			Bed Rm.	3		
1.5			Baths	1.75 + R/I	+	360.00
--			Fam. Rm.	300 x 3.5	= +	1050.00
--			Rec. Rm.	--		
4			Carp/drapes	6	= +	200.00
--			Fireplace	--		
H/F, Disp, R/O, D/W			Kit App.	H/F, Disp, R/O, D/W		
yes			A/C	yes		
2 car att			Garage	2 car B/I	-	1200.00
same			Lot	same		
(new around) better			Loc	good	-	1,000.00
good			Cond	good		
1			Drapes	5 = 4x50	= +	200.00
			TOTALS			$36,171.15

KIRBY - YOWELL , REALTORS   OLD MILL CENTER

BALL REAL ESTATE
Locally Owned

REAL ESTATE - MULTIPLE LISTING SERVICE - INSURANCE
626 North 108th Court,   Omaha, Nebraska. 68154   (402) 496-2000

COMPETITIVE MARKET ANALYSIS FORM

Date 11/4/76

COMPARABLES				SUBJECT PROPERTY			
1. ADDRESS 8537				Decatur Street			
1200	=	33,000	Sq. Ft.	1232	=		33,880
3			Bed Rm.	3			
1.5			Baths	1.75	+ R/I =	+	360
--			Fam. Rm.	300 x 3.5	=	+	1050
--			Rec. Rm.	--			
4			Carp/~~drapes~~	6	=	+	200
			Fireplace	--			
H/F, R/O, D/W			Kit App.	H/F, R/O, D/W, Disp		+	50
yes			A/C	yes			
2 car Bi			Garage	2 car BI			
same			Lot	same			
Newer homes - better			Loc	good		-	750
			Cond.				
2			Drapes	5	= + 3 x 50 =	+	150
yes			Tool Shed	No	=	-	200
242' x 2.4 = + 580.80			Fence	No	=	-	580.80
			TOTALS				$34,159.20
2. ADDRESS							
			Sq. Ft.				
			Bed Rm.				
			Baths				
			Fam. Rm.				
			Rec. Rm.				
			Carp/drapes				
			Fireplace				
			Kit App.				
			A/C				
			Garage				
			Lot				
			Loc				
			Cond				
			TOTALS				

BALL REAL ESTATE
Locally Owned

KIRBY - YOWELL , REALTORS   OLD MILL CENTER

REAL ESTATE - MULTIPLE LISTING SERVICE - INSURANCE
626 North 108th Court,   Omaha, Nebraska. 68154   (402) 496-2000

'ESTIMATE OF SELLER'S EXPENSE AND NET'

DATE___November 4, 1976_____

APPROX. SETTLEMENT DATE__January 1, 1977__

NAME_Mr. and Mrs._____

ADDRESS_____Decatur Street_____

SALES PRICE		35,000
PRO-RATED TAXES		
~~PRO-RATED RENTS~~ 6 Mo's	472.55	
REFUND OF ESCROWS ?		472.55
		35,472.55
LESS		
DOCUMENTARY STAMPS	38.50	
ESTIMATED ABSTRACTING	70.00	
TO RECORD & SHOW RELEASE OF MTGE.	7.25	
LOAN DISCOUNT POINTS 1%	315.00	
FEE FOR PROFESSIONAL SERVICES 7%	2450.00	
FHA OR VA APPRAISAL	---	
TAXES DUE	----	
REPAIR COSTS	---	
PRE-PAYMENT CHARGE ? (Same Co. for Mgt.)	---	
INTEREST PRO-RATED IF ASSUMPTION	---	
OTHER CHARGES Paving expense	2000.00	
TOTAL ESTIMATED EXPENSES		4,880.75
SELLER'S APPROXIMATE NET BEFORE MORTGAGE PAY-OFF		30,591.80
ASSUMING MORTGAGE BALANCE IS APPROXIMATELY		27,000.00
APPROXIMATE NET AFTER MORTGAGE PAY-OFF		$ 3,591.80

10-5 REPORTING COMPARABLES ON SEVERAL PROPERTIES

Dear _____:

As I always do, I go over all comparable sales on all of our proposed listings. You told me to shoot from the hip and I will. Here are the facts . . .

1. Lot at 84th & _____ St.
   If this were to go on the market at $2,500.00 as is + $567.00 assessment and + future paving of $1,800.00 (approximately—150′ × $120.00) that would equal $5,000. People won't pay $5,000 for a lot in this area.

2. Lot at 81st & _____
   I checked the zoning of all the land east of your lot and the zoning is R8—all except the house next to yours. There is a possibility there if Mr. _____ would want to move the house. I couldn't reach Mr. _____; he is out of town on vacation.

3. Lot at 60th & _____ St.
   After checking with numerous sources, it looks like the lot would be worth approximately $3,300.00.

4. Lot at 34th & _____ Street
   I talked to an owner of the other lots in that area, and he says those lots are worth about $500.00. A builder cannot build in a 235 on a 42′ lot—it must be 50′.

5. _____ Street
   I checked comparable homes in the area and they show prices of about $35,000.00 to $36,500.00

6. _____ No. _____ St.
   Comparables show a sale price would be about $37,500.00

Mr. _____, I don't feel that we could honestly give a 100% sales effort on your lots unless the prices come close to these comparables.

I will be glad to discuss this information with you further should you so desire.

Sincerely,

10-6 MODEL RESIDENTIAL REPORT TO A CORPORATION

Dear _____:

I am enclosing my appraisal report that your company requested.

RESIDENTIAL APPRAISAL REPORT
APPRAISAL DATE June 10, 19___
PROPERTY ADDRESS 16827 Street
City, State

A. APPRAISED VALUE

1. PRESENT FAIR MARKET VALUE OF PROPERTY (INCLUDE LOT) $36,000

2. LAND OR LOT VALUE $ 5,040

3. ESTIMATED MONTHLY RENTAL $ 325

B. LOCATION OF PROPERTY AND NEIGHBORHOOD

Property is in a fine location. It is close to elementary, junior and senior schools. Shopping and transportation are close by. The value of the homes in this neighborhood range from $30,000–$38,000.

C. ASSESSED VALUE AND TAXES

	LAND		IMPROVEMENTS	
	ASSESSED VALUE	ANNUAL TAXES	ASSESSED VALUE	ANNUAL TAXES
CITY	$ 5,040	$ 172.34	$ 28,560	$ 976.6(
COUNTY				
OTHER				
TOTAL	$ 5,040	$ 172.34	$ 28,560	$ 976.6(

D. UTILITIES

Gas, Water, Sewer and Paving are all in and paid for.

E. DESCRIPTION OF LOT AND IMPROVEMENTS PLOT
    PLAN
    Lot 27, Block 15, Bel ____, ____ ____, ____, ____
    70' × 137' Size of Lot

F. BUILDING EXTERIOR
    Steel Siding

G. BUILDING INTERIOR
    Beautifully decorated with the latest in modern conveniences:
    air conditioning, disposal, range, and oven, compactor, etc.

SKETCHES

H. COMPARABLE PROPERTIES FOR SALE IN IMME-
    DIATE VICINITY

I. COMPARABLE RECENT SALES IN GENERAL AREA
    11638 ____ ____ Street   36,093
    2114   So.   ____ Street   36,245.43
    ____   ____ 116th   St.   34,516.81

J. FINANCING
    All terms available except land contract

K. GENERAL REMARKS
    Excellent location and well-maintained home.

L. QUALIFICATIONS OF APPRAISER
    M. A. I.
    _____ State Appraiser

                                        Sincerely,

10-7 APPRAISAL LETTER/REPORT FOR CORPORATE PROSPECT

Dear _____:

       I hereby certify that I have personally inspected the property described as Lot _____, _____, an addition to the City of _____, _____ County, _____ also known as _____ Street.

       In my opinion as of this date the Market Value is $45,300.

       Market Value is the price that a property will bring in a competitive market under all conditions requisite to a fair sale, which would result from negotiations between a buyer and a seller, each acting prudently, with knowledge, and without undue stimulus. Opinion of Market Value was determined primarily on the third adjusted comparables submitted.

       The property was appraised as a whole, owned in fee simple and unencumbered, subject to the contingent and limited conditions outlined herein.

CONTINGENT AND LIMITING CONDITIONS:

       I assume no responsibility for matters legal in nature, nor do I render any opinion as to the title, which is assumed to be marketable. The property is appraised as though under responsible ownership.

       I am not required to give testimony or appear in court because of having made this appraisal with reference to the property in question unless arrangements have been previously made therefor.

       I assume that there are no hidden or unapparent conditions of the property, subsoil or structures that would render it more or less valuable. I assume no responsibility for such conditions or for engineering that might be required to discover such factors.

Information, estimates and opinions furnished to me and contained in this report were obtained from sources considered reliable and believed to be true and correct. However, no responsibility for accuracy can be assumed by me.

CERTIFICATION:

I hereby certify that I have no interest, present or contemplated, in the property appraised and that neither the employment to make the appraisal, nor the compensation, is contingent on the value of the property. I certify that I have personally inspected the property and that, according to the best of my knowledge and belief, all statements and information in the report are true and correct and that no information has knowingly been withheld. This appraisal report is subject to the contingent and limiting conditions contained herein.

Sincerely,

10-8 MODEL REPORT INCLUDING VALUE ESTIMATE AND LIMITING CONDITIONS

Dear _____:

In compliance with your request, I have appraised and herewith submit my report on the following property:

Local Address: _____ NE _____
　　　　　　　　Street　　　　　　　　　_____,

_____, _____

Legal description: Lot Thirty-one (31) _____
　　　　　　　　　　_____Place, an Official
　　　　　　　　Plat　　　in　　　　_____
　　　　　　　　　　_____County,

_____.

The purpose of the appraisal is to estimate the fair market value of the Fee Simple Title for mortgage loan purposes as of March 24, 19___; both in an "as is" condition and "as required" with repairs completed in a workmanship-like manner. (See attached repair schedule).

Market value is defined as "the price a property will bring in a competitive market under all conditions requisite to a fair sale, which would result from negotiations between a buyer and a seller, each acting prudently, with knowledge and without undue stimulus."

The property appraised includes the real estate comprising the land, land improvements and buildings, but does not include the furnishings or other personal contents.

Valuation Estimate

In considering all of the data and factors involved in this appraisal and based upon a personal inspection, it is my opinion that the market value of the real estate as of the date stated is:

$33,000—"As Is"
$36,000—"As Repaired"

The data and reasoning supporting the value conclusion reached, which may include comparable sales approach, the income approach and the cost approach which have been by reason of this report, excluded; but information is retained in the appraiser's file.

Limiting Conditions

It is assumed that the legal description furnished is correct and that the improvements are entirely located on the property described. No survey has been made.

This appraisal is to be used in whole and not in part. The appraiser, by reason of this report, is not required to give testimony in court unless previously arranged. No responsibility is assumed for matters of a legal nature, nor is any opinion on title rendered.

I assume that there are no hidden or unapparent conditions of the property or subsoil that would render it more or less valuable. I assume no responsibility for such conditions or for engineering that might be required to discover such factors.

Information, estimates and opinions furnished to me and contained in this report were obtained from sources considered reliable and believed to be true and correct. However, no responsibility for accuracy can be assumed by me. Neither all nor any part of the contents of this report, or copy thereof, shall be used for any purpose by any but the client without previous written consent of the appraiser and/or the client; nor shall it be conveyed by any, including the client to the public through advertising, public relations, news, sales or other media, without the written consent and approval of the author, particularly as to value conclusions, the identity of the appraiser or a firm with which he is connected or any reference to any professional society or institute or any initialed designations conferred upon the appraiser.

Appraiser's Certification

I hereby certify that I have no interest, present or contemplated, in the property, and that neither the employment to make the appraisal, nor the compensation, is contingent on the value of the property. I certify that, according to my knowledge and belief, all statements and information in the written appraisal retained in my files are true and correct subject to the assumption and limiting conditions contained therein (or attached hereto) and that no information has knowingly been withheld.

Respectfully submitted,

10-9 SHORT APPRAISAL REPORT LETTER

Dear _____:

      Pursuant to your request I have inspected the property commonly known as _____ N. _____, _____, _____, and legally described as follows: The West 60 feet of the North 180 feet in Block 49, Amended Map of _____ School Land Addition to City of _____. Except the South 10 feet conveyed to the City of _____ for street purposes.

      Said inspection was made to estimate "Current Fair Market Value.' "Current Fair Market Value" is defined as the amount that the seller could obtain from his property in its present condition and location, after time for negotiation, which is reasonable for the area, and not based on an immediate sale due to unusual circumstances.

      This valuation is subject to the following limiting conditions:

1. The legal description is assumed to be correct.
2. We assume no responsibility for matters legal in character nor do we render any opinion as to title, which is assumed to be marketable. Any existing liens and encumbrances have been disregarded and the property is valued as though free and clear under responsible ownership.
3. It is assumed that there are no encroachments, zoning violations or restrictions existing on the subject property.
4. Information, estimates and opinions contained in this report are obtained from sources considered reliable, however, no liability for them can be assumed by the undersigned.

Estimated value: Land and Improvements $40,275.00

                    Respectfully submitted,

10-10   LETTER FROM MORTGAGE COMPANY OFFERING USE OF "COMP" BOOKS

Dear _____:

NOW THERE ARE TWENTY-TWO . . .

Twenty-two conveniently located offices anxious to assist appraisers working in the communities we serve.

We are offering, without obligation, access to our comparable sale files.

Our "comp" books contain accurate records of most of the residential properties sold in these areas. These books are maintained according to architectural styling. Within each category, listing sheets are filed according to price and size. Recorded on each sheet is the selling price, date of sale, lot size, taxes, size of rooms, etc. In many instances, the square footage and a picture of the property is also available.

If we can be of assistance, please call us.

Sincerely,

10-11 INFORMAL REPORT ON APPRAISAL

Dear Mr. _____:

Thank you for the opportunity to inspect your property. The home, as you are aware, needs some "cleaning-up" to show properly and thus obtain a sale at top market dollar.

Basing my conclusion on a careful analysis and physical inspection of the property, I find that the replacement value is approximately $135,000. This figure is based upon allowances for depreciation which is an inherent factor in the appraisal of any property. With this figure as a starting point, I then considered the supply and demand for similar homes in the area.

Weighing all of these factors, I arrived at a fair market value of between $125,000 and $130,000.

My recommendation is to offer the property for sale at $129,500.

I would like to call your attention to the fact that not only are we members of the Multiple Listing Service of the _____Board of Realtors, but we also are members of several national referral services.

We at _____, Realtors will be pleased to represent you in the sale of this property. I will call you on Friday, December 12 to discuss this further.

With kindest regards from _____, Realtors, I am

Sincerely yours,

10-12 REPORTING APPRAISED VALUE FOR PURPOSES OF TRADE—BEFORE AGREEMENT

Dear _____:

In my opinion as of this date, your home should sell for between $36,000 and $36,500. My opinion is based primarily on the three adjusted comparables enclosed as well as on other homes we have sold in the area.

Based on our appraisal, Mr. _____ will agree to execute a guaranteed trade agreement in the amount of $32,000. If your home is not sold after being exposed to the market for 90 days, we will take it in trade for $32,000 less the normal seller's costs such as state documentary stamps, pro-rated taxes to possession, mortgage release, and bringing an abstract to date.

Respectfully submitted,

10-13   LETTER WITH GUARANTEE TRADE AGREEMENT

Dear _____:

Enclosed you will find our company's guarantee to you. It is as follows:

_____ _____ Realtors will guarantee you $31,000 on _____ North _____ Street less the normal seller's expenses which include your furnishing our company with an abstract brought to date, the revenue stamps, and taxes pro-rated to possession. _____ _____ Realtors will pay you the guarantee after exposing your home to the market place for 120 days from March 13, _____. If your home sells prior to the 120 days for more than $31,000 net, it is understood you are free to accept the offer and will receive the proceeds just as if it were an ordinary sale less the normal expenses including our commission.

If you have any questions, feel free to call me.

Sincerely,

_____President

_____Vice President

Chapter 11

Model Letters for Dealing With Banks and Other Financial Institutions

Buyers and sellers, agents and lenders all have to work smoothly to put together real estate transactions. These letters will help you deal more effectively with the many financing matters you face every day . . .

11-1 MODEL INTENT-TO-SELL LETTER TO MORTGAGE COMPANY

Subject: "Letter-of-Intent" from Mortgagor notifying the Mortgagee, in compliance with 30 day advance-notice provision of Mortgage, of the intention to pay off the remaining principal balance due on Mortgage Loan #_____

Dear _____:

Our property is currently being offered for sale. In the event of a firm sale, it is our intention to pay off this mortgage.

You are hereby given permission to provide the following preliminary information concerning my property, the indebtedness and insurance to a representative of _____ Co., Inc., Realtors.

_____, 19__   _____
Date   Owner

_____

1. Loan Identification # _____ Original term of loan?

   _____ Date loan originated? _____

2. Current loan balance? _____ As of (date) _____

   Res. Acct. balance $_____ Shortage? _____

   How much _____

3. Total monthly payment $_____ Amt. to Princ. & Int.

   _____

Amt. to Taxes $_____ Amt. to Hazard Ins. $_____

Amt., if any, to Mortg. Ins. $_____ Int. rate on loan

_____

4. Payments current?_____ If not, how much to bring current?

5. Interest is paid to _____ Taxes $ _____

   Fully Paid? _____

6. Amt. of Ins. Coverage $_____ Premium

   $_____ for _____ years

   Date of expiration _____Company _____

   Agent _____Policy # _____

7. Assumption fee $_____ Requirements for loan assumption by new owner: _____

   _____

8. What will the prepayment penalty be if paid in full? _____
Please return to:

_____ Co. Inc., Realtors   _____
                                   Lenders Representative
                                   Sincerely,

11-2 LETTER TO MORTGAGE COMPANY EXPLAINING PURCHASER'S ASSETS

Dear _____:

We have an earnest deposit from Mr. & Mrs. _____ of $5,000.00. The purchasers also have $5,000.00 in cash value on a life insurance policy. They are going to use this amount to reduce their mortgage to $32,500.00 instead of $37,500.00 as originally planned. The $5,000.00 from the cash value of life insurance will be used to increase the initial investment.

Serviceably yours,

11-3 EXPLANATION OF ELIGIBILITY FOR LOW-INCOME GOVERNMENT SUBSIDY

Dear _____:

I am well aware that for a 3-bedroom home the limit on the 235 program is $_____. I have also heard that there have been exceptions to this rule. I would certainly appreciate it if an exception could be worked out for this family. They meet all of the other main requirements:

1. Their income after the deduction for each child is within the limit of $_____.
2. Their savings are far below the $_____ limit.
3. They are tyring to stay within the $_____ limit on price, but they cannot.

During the course of house hunting for Mr. & Mrs. _____ we showed them eighteen to twenty homes. We took them into five of these to inspect, but none of these fit the needs of a family of eight persons. All of the above homes were in the $_____ price range. We cannot find this family adequate housing in the lower 235 limit.

In order to find a suitable home, we went into a higher price range and looked at eight or ten others before finding a home that properly fit the needs of this family. We most certainly feel that this family is worthy of the low-income government subsidy program.

Sincerely,

11-4   REQUEST FOR LOAN PAY-OFF LETTER

Dear _____:

    We have sold the home of Mr. _____ at _____ Street, _____, _____, Lot 16, Block 2, _____ Valley. We were advised by _____ Co. that Mr. _____ now handles this _____ Life account.

    Closing will be March 31, 19__, and we need a payoff letter and the paid tax receipts from you, as the purchaser has obtained a new loan. Please return these quickly because closing must be on March 31.

    Thank you for your cooperation.

                                   Sincerely,

11-5   ANSWERING A REQUEST FOR PAYMENT INFORMATION FROM MORTGAGOR

Dear _____:

    Enclosed is a copy of our cancelled check for the December payment and Loan Fee on the described property. This was mailed December 11, along with a letter of explanation, containing the _____ Loan number. Since then the recorded deed (copy) has been sent to you. I hope this will be of assistance to you.

                                   Sincerely,

11-6 ADVISING MORTGAGOR OF COMPLIANCE WITH V.A. REQUIREMENTS

Dear _____:

Per our conversation on January 19, 19___, concerning _____No. _____ Street, I am enclosing a sheet describing what work will be done in order to qualify this property as a duplex for a V.A. Loan.

The work to be done is as follows:

1. Basement apartment will be eliminated—rooms will be used for a family room and storage.
2. First floor apartment will be converted to one large apartment. Apartment to the north will be converted to bedrooms.
3. Second floor apartment will be converted to one large apartment.
4. Third floor sleeping rooms will be used for an attic to store items.

If there is need for further explanation, please let me know.

Sincerely,

11-7 TO MORTGAGE COMPANY IN REGARDS TO INSURANCE POLICY

Dear _____:

The insurance policy that I wrote for Mr. and Mrs. _____ amounted to $70.60. Fifty dollars of the amount will come from the escrow account and I have enclosed a company check for the difference. I talked to Mr. _____ concerning this matter. He said that because Mr. & Mrs. _____ were a little short of funds and since the escrow balance was approximately $100.00 higher than needed, that there would be no problem.

When it is convenient, please remit to me the total amount of the homeowner's policy. Enclosed is a copy of the application for the policy, and I will send the original copy of the policy when it arrives.

Sincerely yours,

11-8   PROSPECTIVE PURCHASER'S EXPLANATION OF DEBTS TO MORTGAGOR

Dear _____:

Ref: Mr.   &   Mrs.   _____   _____.

_____ No. _____ Avenue

    I was told by Mr. _____ of the F.H.A. Office in _____ to state my present debt obligation and to obtain from the _____ Electronics Company an estimate of overtime that I have worked since joining them as an employee. As I stated in my first letter, we had extraordinary medical expenses four years ago, and I also was unemployed since _____ Aircraft Plant cut back on their executive personnel.

    These are my debt obligations and the way in which I am paying them:

1. Hospital and Doctor. This debt is approximately $2,700.00 and I am paying $20.00 per week.
2. Oil bill. $500.00 originally. I am paying this as quickly as I possibly can. I now owe $149.00.
3. Car. I have one payment left amounting to $150.00. This will be paid by February 20, _____.

    I feel that with an income averaging $2,000.00 per month, I would have no trouble meeting my housing and other personal obligations.

    Thank you.

                        Sincerely,

11-9 "THANK YOU" NOTE TO LOAN OFFICER

Dear _____:

The purchase of a new home and the closing of the loan should always be a happy occasion for the buyers. The pleasant and efficient manner in which you handled the closing of the loan for Mr. & Mrs. _____ yesterday is most appreciated. It added much to the enjoyment of the occasion.

We are most grateful to you for all your assistance.

Kindest regards.

Sincerely yours,

11-10 MODEL LOAN INFORMATION LETTER TO MORTGAGE COMPANY

Dear _____:

　　　　We are placing our property on the market for sale and would greatly appreciate you mailing in the enclosed envelope, attention of Mr. _____ and _____, Realtors, _____ Rd., _____, _____, the following information regarding our loan which we have with your company:

NAME _____　　ACCOUNT NO. _____

ADDRESS _____

　　　　We would be most grateful for your trouble and will endeavor to influence any buyers to make their loan with you.

1. Balance due $ _____　　10. Deed Book _____
　　　　　　　　　　　　　　　　　　　Page _____
2. As of _____
　　　　　　　　　　　　　　　　11. Do you have survey _____
3. Original date of loan _____
　　　　　　　　　　　　　　　　12. Monthly Escrow FHA
4. Original amount $_____　　　　Ins. _____
5. Term (years) _____　　13. Total Monthly Pmt.
　　　　　　　　　　　　　　　　　　(PITI) $ _____
6. Type of Loan _____
　　　　　　　　　　　　　　　　14. Present Escrow Bal. _____
7. Interest Rate _____
　　　　　　　　　　　　　　　　15. Ins. with _____
8. City and School tax _____

9. St. and County Tax _____

16. Exp. date of Hazard Ins.

      ———————————

17. Amt. of Hazard Ins. ——

18. Prepayment privilege ——

19. Payoff penalty ————

20. Transfer fee $————

21. Credit report required
    NO ————————————

22. Interest rate same NO %
    YES ———— ———— %

In the event your company requires a loan payoff notice and since we expect to sell in the next 30 to 60 days, please consider this letter as such a notice.

Thank you for your courtesy,

11-11 MODEL APPRAISAL REPORT TO BANK ACTING AS TRUSTEE

Dear _____:

In my opinion as of this date, _____ Hanover would sell between $37,500 and $38,500, and the financing would most likely be FHA or VA (i.e., low down payment type of loan with discount points to the seller—probably 3 points). FHA or VA would most likely require the garage to be painted at least on two sides where it is peeling.

This home is immaculate and should sell well at this time. It does have an older type oil furnace, and old fashion bath, and an electric water heater which will be resistance items to many buyers. Also, the neighborhood values are trending downward. This home would probably rent for $350 to $375, but if a tenant did not keep the condition of the home up as it is now, or if the neighborhood values continue downward, the market value could be substantially lower in the future.

I base my opinion primarily on three comparable homes that have sold recently. After adjusting them to compensate for the various features that_____ Hanover either has or does not have, I came up with an average price of $37,750, a low of $37,250 and a high of $38,250.

If you were to put the home on the market, I would recommend a list price of $38,950.00. I would be hesitant to rent the home because of the reasons given.

Sincerely,

11-12 NOTIFICATION OF INCREASE IN FEES FOR APPRAISALS

Dear _____:

I appreciate the past appraisal business from your bank, especially in regards to residential property and small investment property. However, because of the time involved in doing them properly, please be advised that my minimum fee for this type of appraisal in the future will be $75.00–$100.00, depending on where the property is located and the time necessary to do the appraisal.

Sincerely,

11-13   USED WITH BANK OFFICER—INTERIM FINANCING

Dear _____:

Enclosed is a copy of the guarantee that we gave Mrs. _____. If you need more information, please let me know. We already have an offer on Mrs. _____'s home for more than our guarantee, but it was a little lower than Mrs. _____ should accept at this time. The prospective purchasers may come up and take the counter. We don't know yet. If they do, Mrs. _____ will still need interim financing. Her purchase in _____ should close during the week of March 29th thru April 2nd.

This written guarantee has worked successfully for us and the client in 95% of the cases—19 out of 20. I feel that the home we are guaranteeing for Mrs. _____ is one of the best we have ever guaranteed.

Thank you for your past cooperation, and I will be in touch as soon as her home sells.

Sincerely,

11-14 ASKING FOR SPECIAL CONSIDERATION FROM LOAN OFFICER

Dear _____:

    I certainly appreciated your time and consideration during our phone conversation yesterday. I just wanted to reiterate the position I am in by hand. I know that it will be a squeeze, but I am sure we can accomplish this. I will do anything that I can do to help.

    We must close Mr. & Mrs. _____'s loan Friday morning in order that I can wire the money to Mr. and Mrs. _____ early Friday afternoon so they can close their loan in _____, Colorado. My sellers must close in Colorado by 4:30 P.M. Friday. There is a contingency clause in their offer to purchase, and Friday is their last day to close or they will lose the home.

    We have had many delays that were not the fault of the seller, so I feel that extra effort should be exerted in this closing by your mortgage company and all parties concerned.

    Thank you for your past cooperation, and I will do anything that would be helpful.

                        Sincerely yours,

11-15   PAPERS TO GO OUT-OF-TOWN

Dear _____ :

It appears that Mr. and Mrs. _____ will not be here for our closing that is set for July 20, 19__. It doesn't happen very often, but it will be necessary for your mortgage loan company to send all the necessary papers to the purchaser for their signature in _____, Washington.

I talked to my sellers yesterday, and they must have their proceeds from the sale by August 29, 19__. They are moving into _____ Manor on September 3, 19__, and they must pay their fee one month prior to moving in.

It appears that we have plenty of time to successfully complete this task, and the purchaser is receptive to this arrangement.

Thank you again and I have set the closing with your loan officer and the sellers for July 20, 19__.

Sincerely yours,

11-16 BANK AS ESCROW AGENT

Dear _____:

I want to thank you for your prompt action in signing the necessary escrow agreement papers. This transaction has taken seven months to close.

We have the land contract closing set for 2 P.M. on Friday, December 16, 19___. As soon as I receive the proceeds from the purchaser and remit them to the seller, I will personally hand deliver the executed papers to you.

Thank you again for your prompt action.

Sincerely yours,

11-17   A PRE-PAYMENT PENALTY IS SOLVED

Dear _____:

      I certainly appreciate the fine work you did for Mr. and Mrs. _____. We and they are certainly thankful for your efforts with _____ Federal concerning the pre-payment clause on their note for the house at _____ South _____ Street. This was one of those incidents that could have erupted into a very unhappy situation. It taught us that verbal communications mean nothing, and that purchasers are not aware of pre-payment charges when mortgages are paid in full. They are told about this matter, but they simply don't remember. Thanks again for your hard work. You certainly went beyond the call of duty.

      When you are in the _____ area, please drop in and visit with us.

                        Sincerely yours,

Chapter 12

Dealing With Legal Problems and Attorneys Through Effective Model Letters

You can be of much greater service to your clients if you work smoothly and effectively with attorneys. The following 15 model letters will help you deal with attorneys on key transactions, problems and opportunities. . . .

12-1   MODEL LETTER TO ATTORNEY REQUESTING ESTATE PROPERTY LISTING

Dear _____:

   I spoke to your secretary, Mrs. _____, and she said that I should send you a letter in reference to the property located at 48th and _____—a property in the _____ estate you are representing.

   I received a call from Mr. _____, a past client of mine and the executor for the estate, stating that he would prefer that I be the listing agent for this transaction when it takes place.

   Your secretary mentioned that I should call you in the first week of April, since you would not be back until then. I would certainly appreciate the opportunity to be the agent for the estate in the sale of this property.

   Thank you and I will call you when you return.

                                        Sincerely,

12-2 SHORT APPRAISAL REPORT TO ATTORNEY FOR ESTATE

Dear _____:

Mrs. _____, a past client of yours and mine, requested that I conduct an appraisal on her 160 acres near _____ and send you the report of value. The reason for this appraisal is for estate purposes.

I have looked at and collected data on the 160 acres which is approximately ¾ mile north of Interstate _____ on Highway _____, south of _____, Arizona.

In my opinion, the market value of this land is approximately $800.00 (Eight Hundred Dollars) per acre. Mrs. _____ said that you did not need the complete appraisal—just a letter stating the value. If you should find it necessary to have the appraisal report, you can obtain it either from her or from me.

If I can be of further service, please call me.

Sincerely yours,

12-3 COVER NOTE FOR TRANSFER OF CLOSING FORMS

Dear _____:

As per our telephone conversation, I am enclosing the following items:

1. Closing statement for Mr. & Mrs. _____ _____
2. _____ Mortgage Company's costs.
3. Title Binder
4. Seller's statement showing that all items on the title binder and the F.H.A. appraisal sheet are to be paid by the seller.

If there are any questions, please call. Thank you.

Sincerely,

12-4 COVER NOTE FOR SENDING AGREEMENT OF SALE AND DEED TO ATTORNEY

Dear _____:

Enclosed is a copy of the Agreement of Sale and the deed on the above-captioned property which the purchasers have asked us to forward to you to prepare for their settlement.

Should you have any questions regarding the above please contact Mr. _____ at our _____ office.

Very truly yours,

12-5 REQUESTING ATTORNEY TO PROCEED WITH TITLE SEARCH

Dear _____:

Please proceed with the title search preparatory to final settlement on above-captioned property which is being purchased by Mr. _____.

A copy of the Agreement of Sale and deed are enclosed.

Surveys have been ordered from _____ & _____ for delivery to your office.

Mortgage will be granted by _____ in the amount of $_____ and will be closed in accordance with their usual procedure.

Should you have any questions regarding the above, please contact Mr. _____ at our _____ Street office.

Very truly yours,

12-6 MODEL LETTER REQUESTING EXAMINATION OF ABSTRACT OF TITLE

Dear _____:

You will be receiving an Abstract of Title to examine. The information is outlined below.

DATE ABSTRACT ORDERED _____

ABSTRACT COMING FROM _____

EXAMINE FOR _____

SELLER _____

ADDRESS OF PROPERTY _____

LEGAL DESCRIPTION _____

_____

TYPE OF SALE _____

SEND OPINION TO _____

COPY TO _____

SALESMAN _____

OTHER _____

_____

_____

We are enclosing a copy of the Purchase Agreement. Would you please notify us when it is ready?

Sincerely,

12-7 A COMPLETE EXPLANATION OF CLOSING COSTS

Dear _____:

As requested per our conversation this morning, this letter and closing statements will explain all the items completely.

Mrs. _____ will receive $348.17 less than originally stated. Let me explain. I am not counting the special assessments on the sewer and water, and the back taxes. These items were not known to me until I received the title binder on September 10. These three items amounted to $2,701.20.

I am basing my figures on the other remaining items. The breakdown is as follows:

Item	Original Statement	Pres. Statement	Cr.
Pro-Rata Taxes	$ 56.84	$ 74.80	$ 17.96
Title Expense	35.00 (approx)	27.63	7.37
Seller's discount	742.00	606.00	136.00
Repair Work (F.H.A.—bottom of sheet)	755.00	610.00	145.00
Rent: $150.00 per month May 18-June 18 June 18-July 18	Not included	450.00 (already paid)	450.00
July 18-Aug. 18 Rent (Present Closing Statement) $150.00 per month Aug. 18-Sept. 18 Sept. 18-Oct. 15 (approx)		385.00	285.00

Examination by

_____ & _____   Not included   27.50   27.50
                                                                        (debit)

                                                                      $1,013.83
                                                                       (credit)

Thus $1,362.00 (Plumbing and Electrical requirements by F.H.A.) less $1,013.83=$348.17.

Even with the requirements that the plumbing, electrical and heating be adequate and in working order, Mrs. _____ is actually receiving only $348.17 less than the original amount—not counting special assessments via title binder which, as explained before, were not known.

Let me also explain two items. We must count the rent as a credit because this property, without the sewer connection, would not have been rentable. The septic system was backing up daily. Also, even if Mrs. _____ would have rented the property, she soon would have been charged with bringing the electrical and plumbing system up to date. As you know, the city inspectors are checking every older property and require that the structure's heating, plumbing and wiring meet city code. So the $1,362.00 figure for the plumbing and electrical would have been required. I also want to point out that petitions are being passed out in this area for paving. The purchaser is responsible for this.

Mr. _____, I firmly believe that Mrs. _____ is fortunate in disposing of this property at the new statement figure. On the F.H.A. appraisal, these requirements were present and on our purchase agreement dated May 18, 19__, I stated in #5 that all stipulations of the F.H.A. conditional appraisal must be satisfied by the seller.

If you have any questions, please call me. We are ready to close as soon as the deed returns. These final figures are as of this date. The closing date could change some items.

Sincerely,

12-8   BRIEF HOME APPRAISAL REPORT FOR AN ATTORNEY

Dear _____:

We have inspected the home at _____ St. and found it to be an exceptionally fine two bedroom, custom ranch of 862 square feet. The home is located in a good neighborhood of homes of comparable value.

Checking comparables, we found a two bedroom ranch at _____ St. which sold in the past year for $32,250.00. This home is some 200 square feet larger and has central air conditioning. Based on this and other factors we feel the _____ home should be listed for $31,950.00 and expected to sell for $31,000.00 or $31,500.00.

We wish to thank you for this opportunity, and hope we can be of assistance to you and your client.

Very sincerely yours,

12-9   REQUESTING INVESTOR REFERRALS FROM AN ATTORNEY

Dear _____:

      I have talked to you about two choice properties that we have listed. (I am enclosing copies of these listings.) These are two very fine properties, Bill. If you have any clients who would be interested in them, please feel free to call me anytime.

                                       Sincerely,

12-10   LISTING DESCRIPTION FOR TOWN LEGAL DEPARTMENT

Dear _____:

Mr. _____, a past client of mine, advised me to send this letter to your attention because the legal department of the city has the final say in the acquisition of property for city use. I have enclosed a proposal describing property that I believe may be of use to the city.

I first contacted Mr. _____, Chief of Police, and he stated that he could not render the decision on these properties. He did say that the city was looking for properties in this area for specific purposes. He suggested that I contact you.

It is my understanding that the city has received federal grants for the purpose of acquiring property in this section of the city for police usage and for recreational purposes. The properties I have listed in the proposal might meet these two needs.

These properties, as described on the enclosed proposal sheet, are in good repair. If they can be used by some department of the city, I would certainly recommend further consideration of this proposal.

Thank you, and if you have any questions, please call.

Sincerely yours,

PROPOSAL

Location: 1502-04-05-08 _____ Street
Type Building: Brick
Buildings: 1. <u>1502-04</u>

> Central Air
> Cabinet Gas Furnace (Installed 19___)
> 220 V. wiring (In 19___)
> Stool
> Basement
> New roof—3 year guarantee (up to 19___)

2. 1506 _____ Street
   Cabinet Gas Furnace (Installed 19__)
   220 V. wiring (In 19__)
   Stool
   Basement
   New roof (same as above)
3. 1508 _____ Street
   Cabinet Gas Furnace
   220 V. wiring (In 19__)
   Stool
   Basement
   New roof (same as above)

Terms: Lease—Purchase at $287.50 per month for 6 years.
           No interest charge
           After 6 years, buildings would belong to the City of
           _____—free and clear

Also in this package Mr. _____ will provide a lot at 25th & _____ for five years at no expense. The lot size is 200′ × 200′. It might be ideal for a playground for children.

12-11 A THANK YOU NOTE FOR ATTORNEY'S ASSISTANCE

Good Morning Mr. _____:

     We appreciate the pleasant and efficient manner in which you handled the closing of the property at _____ _____ Lane, purchased by Mr. & Mrs. _____.

     It was a pleasure to work with you in the closing of this transaction and we just wanted to say, "Thanks."

     Kindest regards.

                           Sincerely yours,

12-12   ANOTHER NOTE OF APPRECIATION FOR AN ATTORNEY'S SERVICES

Dear _____:

This letter is to express my appreciation for your cooperation in connection with the sale of Mr. and Mrs. _____'s home located at _____ _____ Drive, _____, _____.

The role of a Realtor is so much simpler in matters of this type when the attorneys are as familiar as you are with real estate transactions.

If at any time in the future, we can be of service to you or to your clients in connection with any real estate, insurance or property management matter, I sincerely hope you will not hesitate to call upon us.

Very truly yours,

12-13   GRIEVANCE COMMITTEE REPLY TO ATTORNEY'S INQUIRY

Dear _____:

Your letter of September 11, 19__, in which you inquired about the procedure used by the _____ Real Estate Company on the above mentioned sale, was referred to the Grievance Committee of the _____ Real Estate Board, as stipulated in the By-laws.

The committee met on September 20. After thoroughly investigating your complaint, they unanimously agreed that no unethical practice occurred on the part of _____ Real Estate, or the agents thereof, and all legal documents were properly filled out.

We therefore find no guilt on the part of _____ Real Estate Company, or any of its agents, in purchasing the property from Mr. and Mrs. _____.

Sincerely yours,

12-14   ANOTHER MODEL REPLY TO AN ATTORNEY'S INQUIRY

Dear _____:

The letter that you sent to the attention of _____ Realty, _____ Realty, and the Multiple Listing Service of _____ with reference to Mr. _____ has been thoroughly examined by our Board's Grievance Committee.

The Grievance Committee has recommended that this matter be turned over to the President of our Multiple Listing Service, Mr. _____ _____.

We recommend to Mr. _____ that these two firms be contacted and that he investigate the circumstances of this transaction. This problem could be, and more than likely is, a legal problem. We cannot determine this because our function is not legal but ethical.

Sincerely,

12-15   RESPONSE TO AN ATTORNEY'S REQUEST TO TERMINATE A LISTING

Dear _____:

I did appreciate your call concerning Mr. and Mrs. _____'s property at _____ Street that we have been authorized to sell.

I have checked with our listing agent and have investigated his activities. I am completely confident that our agent is doing an excellent job.

It appears to me that the problem lies with Mr. _____. He is very unhappy with his transfer and it seems he is using us as a way to vent his anger.

Our agent has spent much time trying to market this home, and we have spent much money advertising the property. We are paid for our time, and I am not, therefore, able to release the listing. We have a completely legal contract and we are trying very hard to sell the home.

We will do our very best to market this home for Mr. and Mrs. _____, and to obtain the highest possible market value.

Sincerely,

Chapter 13

Model Letters That Motivate
Real Estate Salesmen To Sell

Informed and "geared up" sales agents will list more, sell more and earn more. Here are 14 model letters and memos that can help salesmen do just that . . .

13-1 MODEL LETTER OF APPRECIATION

Good Morning ——————:

    Just the shortest of notes to congratulate you on having completed your ——————th year with —————— Company.

    It has been great having you aboard. Even though the seas have not always been smooth for perfect sailing, we have always been optimistic that the water will be smoother tomorrow. I am confident that our optimism will pay dividends.

    I could not allow this opportunity to go by without thanking you for your loyalty and cooperation. I look forward to working with you in the months and years that lie ahead. I know that with good teamwork, these months and years can be both profitable and enjoyable for both of us.

    With best personal regards.

Sincerely yours,

13-2 AN EFFECTIVE "GET GOING" LETTER TO SALES ASSOCIATES

Dear _____:

Ninety percent of the failures in selling are caused by poor time management. Below is a basic real estate activity day. If used, you have an excellent chance for success. Please employ your own methods, but follow the basics and you will surely see an increase in your production.

The basic schedule is as follows:

TODAY

HE WHO ONLY PLANS IS A DREAMER. HE WHO ONLY WORKS IS A DRUDGE. HE WHO PLANS HIS WORK AND WORKS HIS PLAN IS A CONQUEROR.

Morning	*Afternoon*
1. Sharpen Saw	1. Purchasers (top 6)
2. Tickler File	A. Ours (notebook)
3. See 6 people	B. M.L.S.
(friends, acquaintances,	C. Read Paper
strangers)	D. Drive area (if approp.)
—send note	E. Creative
4. Listing Prospects	2. Purchasers (file)
5. Work Appraisals	A. Ours (notebook)
6. See	B. M.L.S.
A. Owners	C. Read paper
B. Expired listings	D. Drive area (if approp.)
C. Farm Concept— cold	E. Creative
canvas	3. New listings (ours)
7. New listings (ours)	

Evening
1. Appointment(s)
2. Purchasers (top & file)
   A. Notebook (ours)
   B. M.L.S.
   C. Read Paper
   D. Drive area (if approp.)
   E. Creative
3. Call Sellers
4. Advancement (taxes, records, books, etc.)

We will cover this schedule during our next training session for new associates. Everyone is welcomed to attend.

Sincerely,

13-3   INSTRUCTIONAL MEMO TO SALES ASSOCIATES (LISTINGS)

TO: _____

RE: Listings

HOW TO GET STARTED IN SELLING EXISTING RESIDENTIAL REAL ESTATE

If you are going to be successful in selling residential real estate, you must be able to get listings. Invariably the top lister for any company is one of the top salesmen for that company. This business is tough, but much easier if you control property (by having an exclusive listing) rather than trying to control the buyer. I am not saying you should ignore the buyer. On the contrary, you should put yourself in his shoes and try to find a good home for him whether you or your company have the desired listing or not. Successful real estate selling still depends, and always will, on whether you are willing to render quality service and hard work.

Since one of the most important steps in this business is to get listings, where do you start? It is obvious the real estate business is a people-oriented business. You therefore must get listings from people. And the first and best place to start is with your close friends, people whom you know on a first name basis, relatives, and people you are doing or have done business with.

How do you get them to give you listings or listing leads? They must be informed that you are now in the real estate business. Perhaps you can think of a better way, but to me the best way to get started is to sit down and compile a list of the names of the people you know well. Place these names on 3 × 5 cards and file them alphabetically. After you have a comprehensive list made up, compose a friendly letter informing them you are now in the real estate business and with whom you are associated. (The letter should be composed by you so it reflects your style.) Tell them a little bit about your company and let them know you would appreciate any help they might give you. Let them know you are seeking good listings to sell.

What do you do now? Wait for all these people to miraculously call you and give you listing leads and referrals? *NOT ON YOUR LIFE!* Here is where the average new salesmen full of enthusiasm might stop, but you must take the next step and the most important step which is a follow-up with a personal contact. Because of the number of letters you should have sent out, it might be difficult timewise to see all the people on your list in person. However, a personal contact after your letter will be the most effective means of getting people to remember you are now in the real estate business and the name of your company. Your contact should be brief, friendly but businesslike rather than social. Give them your card and perhaps something else such as a baby-sitting card or a calendar and be sure to ask them *to remember you* when they or their friends need real estate help or advice.

If you can't contact each friend on your list in person be sure to at least call each one shortly after your mailing. Don't be pushy or aggressive, but be friendly. Ask them how they are, if they got your letter, and remind them you would appreciate any help or support they can give. You will get some leads right away.

When you get some leads be sure and take the next two steps: 1) follow through on all leads immediately; and 2) get back to the person who gave you the lead, thank him again, and inform him of what progress you made. Even if nothing developed on your first contact, the referrer will be curious how you did. If you don't get back to him, he will feel you took him for granted or didn't really appreciate the leads. The next time he gives out leads, they will go to someone else.

The next step might be to call "for sale by owners." Although it is not easy, this is a good source of listings as most owners don't get the job done and eventually list their homes. The old axiom still holds true—selling is a game of averages. You ask enough people to buy or sell, you will do some business.

In addition to contacting "for sale by owners," you should spend time calling people whose names you get out of the phone book or, if you prefer, call people on certain streets by using the street address telephone directory. When using the telephone book, open to any page and call the people having addresses in areas you would like to work in and ask them if they are thinking about selling their home. If they say "no," ask if they know of anyone else who might be thinking of selling. It is important to have some system for recording these leads and comments and also where the leads came from so you can effectively follow-up.

In addition to contacting new people by telephone, it is important to *see and meet one new person each day face to face*. When you are new to the business you can't expect referrals from past real estate clients because you don't have any. But that doesn't mean you can't get referrals. By letting your friends, relatives, and acquaintances know you are in the business, by cold canvassing and by meeting one new person a day, you can develop referred leads in greater numbers than a person who has been in the business several years and doesn't have an effective plan for getting referrals.

The average new salesman thinks he should just sit down in the office and wait for the public to call. Experienced sales people know this is a sure way to starve. Causing something to happen is what counts, not waiting for something to happen. If you wait for the action, you will soon join the multitude who thought they heard the call of the real estate business only to find out they weren't one of the ones chosen to remain.

Let us assume you have sent your letter of introduction out to people who know you well and have followed it up with a personal visit or at least a telephone call. Let's also assume you are calling at least three to five people out of the phone book or street directory a day. By now you probably have realized that the best quality of leads have come from people who know you and have referred you.

The next step is to establish yourself in an area as a person and company most active in this area. Some people new to real estate spread themselves too thin, trying to cover their whole city plus the whole field of real estate such as selling new and existing homes, leasing, managing, etc. One way to get established in an area is to become an expert in the activities in the area. Know what homes are for sale and for how much, know what homes sold recently and the sale price as well as the terms of the sale; meet the people who work in the area such as the mail man, the milk man, the retail merchants, etc. Canvass the area in person, by mail, and by telephone. (One comment about a general mailing: they are limited in value, especially without a personal follow-up shortly after the mailing.) Put an advertisement in the community news-paper if there is one. Call on the "for sale by owner" ads in this area. When your company lists a property make sure you intro-duce it to the neighbors on the street of the new listing by calling some of them. (A call after the sold sign goes up could lead to another good listing!) Stop and visit people working in their yards. People are interested in their homes and neighborhoods, and will be interested in doing business with you if you're interested in them.

Hand your business cards out frequently and to everyone. Don't assume that because people know you're in real estate they will automatically remember to give you referrals. You have to continually remind them that you need and appreciate referrals.

There are two more excellent sources of business that should be developed. People in the real estate business need to involve themselves in a community activity of some nature. If you look around, most successful people in your city are community-minded. It may mean being an Optimist, a Rotarian, a Big Brother, an Elk, a Shriner, a Boy Scout leader, on a mayor's committee, or with some group that has a community project that interests you. But it means more than having your name appear on the group's membership roster. Too many people join an organization for the sole purpose of getting business, but it doesn't work that way. You have to be an active participant, working for the group's goals. You must share your ideas and use your leadership ability. If you do a good job, the other members will enlist your real estate services themselves or refer you when their friends need real estate service. If you make your living selling real estate, isn't it only normal and right that you should be interested and active in your own community?

The other source that will be a plus businesswise for you is referrals by your fellow Realtors. If you work along with them on Real Estate Board Committees, if you join them at the weekly luncheons and at the Realtors picnic, if you join them at the conventions (both State and, if possible, National), you are bound to become acquainted with some Industrial Realtors, loan people, appraisers, etc., who may recommend your services to one of their friends.

The real estate business is very rewarding but hard work! If you have a plan such as this one and follow up with action you will be successful and will enjoy your chosen profession.

13-4   INSTRUCTIONAL MEMO TO SALES ASSOCIATES (PURCHASERS)

TO: _____

RE: Purchasers

In these few pages let's discuss our purchasing clientele.

You should work diligently with six top purchasers. If you are contacting people as you should, you will quickly know of six good purchasers.

No one can draw a line between listing a property or selling a prospect a property. When you are selling a property to a client, you should also be asking if they or any of their friends or acquaintances might be thinking of selling their property.

If you are listing a property, you should ask if the sellers, their friends or acquaintances might be thinking of purchasing a property. The same driving force that propels you to obtain satisfactory listings should also be the force used to find a satisfactory home for each and every purchasing client. Listed below are a few constructive suggestions that have been found to be successful.

1. Work with only six purchasing clients at one time. Let these clients know that they are your top clients—this helps to build loyalty.
2. Obtain all of the requirements that the purchasing clients must have in the home that they are searching for.
3. Check every possible source in order to find a suitable home for your client. Some of the sources are:
   A. Check your own company listings.
   B. Check listings in your local Multiple Listing Service.
   C. Read the newspaper for homes that are listed with firms that are not in the Multiple Listing Service.
   D. Drive the area in which the client is looking in order to see if there are listings in that area that do not regularly appear in the newspaper.
   E. Drive the area in which the client is looking and jot down

the addresses of homes that seem to meet the needs of the client. By using the cross telephone directory, call the owners of the homes you jotted down and ask them if they might be interested in selling their home.

   F. Call your fellow brokers to see if they might know of a home that they have listed that would meet your client's needs.

   G. Call your friends in the given area and ask them if they know of anyone who might be thinking of selling a home that would meet your client's needs.

4. Build loyalty between your client and yourself. Mention to your client that you can show them any home in the city no matter who has it listed. You cannot keep track of every home in a given area, so ask for their assistance in letting you know if they see or read about a home that they would like to see that you may have missed.

5. When a buying prospect calls, and you learn what he or she wants, immediately look up homes that would meet his needs. After looking up these homes go out personally and see the buyer with the list of homes. Make an appointment to show these homes as soon as possible.

6. When a phone call comes into the office while you are on duty, go for the showing of that property. There are two reasons for this.

   A. You can never sell a home over the phone.

   B. The showing may produce a sale. Even if it doesn't, you, by showing the prospect this home or homes, will know more what the prospect wants and more about the prospect as a person.

7. A buying prospect owes no one loyalty. You must earn loyalty by giving the best service available.

8. When a prospect calls, he or she is usually ready to purchase a home in the near future. Calls are precious—they could mean a $1,100.00 commission to you.

9. When a prospect says that he is in no hurry, you should have a red light that flashes in your mind. In many cases, the "no-hurry" buyer is the one who buys that day or the following week.

10. If you have an excellent showing, but are not able to secure an offer immediately, be sure to get back to that prospect within 24 hours. The 24-hour period seems to be a magic figure from national statistics. People tend to act within this time span.

11. With a good showing, go for the offer at that time. Don't let the prospect give you the old saying—"Let me sleep on it." Go for the offer.

12. If you have a properly listed home, then you will be able to say to the purchasing client—"This is the best home and best priced property in this entire area."

A new associate should never think that because he is new that he cannot immediately begin selling and listing homes like a pro. The new associate has one excellent quality—enthusiasm. With enthusiasm and the knowledge of the basic elements of the business, a rookie can go out and sell successfully.

Don't always equate years in the business with years of successful experience. A lazy salesman may have 10 years of experience, but it may be 1 year experience done 10 times.

After you experience a waning in your initial enthusiasm, you will then have, if you follow the above advice, added knowledge which will bring a stronger, more meaningful and successful enthusiasm.

13-5   INSTRUCTIONAL MEMO TO SALES ASSOCIATES (FINANCING)

TO: _____

RE: Financing

In a tight money market you must use many creative methods to sell your client's property. Please be sure to discuss the following items with your seller.

TIGHT MONEY FINANCING

SELLER

1. Conventional forms of financing
   A. Conventional
   B. MGIC
   C. V.A.
   D. H.H.A.
   —May be possible, but can't promise ☐
   —Discount Points will be very high ☐
2. Land Contract ☐
3. First Mortgage carried by seller. ☐
4. Land Contract for a given period of time—then a balloon payment ☐
5. Loan Assumption ☐—Note possible interest change (not on V.A. or F.H.A.)
6. Loan Assumption with seller carrying a second mortgage. ☐
7. Loan Assumption with second mortgage secured from a savings company. ☐
8. Wrap Around Land Contract—*note:* Call clause could be enforced. ☐
9. Loan Assumption with seller carrying 2nd mortgage with interest only payments for specific period of time—then balloon payment. ☐

I am sure these methods will help you during this period. If you have any questions, please ask me.

Sincerely,

13-6 MODEL LETTER TO GIVE SALES ASSOCIATES A PUSH

Dear _____ :

I'm concerned!

Several of our sellers have said everyone is showing their homes but *our* salespeople. Are we trying to show property each and every day?

Our secretaries, when asked, often tell me they have no idea where our salespeople are. If we can't find you, how can your clients?

_____ has been typing very few competitive market analyses lately. Is anyone working on listings?

What happened to our aggressiveness?

What happened to our competitive spirit?

Do we still have a Positive Mental Attitude?

Is anyone following through with action?

Traditionally we have torn the market up during the last three months of the year. I expect to do that again this year. But we need to get in the habit of working—starting right now, today. Or does everyone have more than enough money to get them through the winter?

I would like to suggest the following challenge to everyone. *There is no reason we can't be at least 10% better than the best of our competition.* That means we must know 10% more; give 10% more service; get 10% more referrals; work 10% harder in our farm areas; have a 10% better card file; have a 10% better comparable sale file.

If each of us works at being 10% better than ever before, our service would truly be the best. Everyone knows what to do—the question is, *Do you really want to do what's necessary?* I believe down deep everyone does and will. Talk is cheap! Let's do it!

Sincerely,

13-7 REVIEW LETTER FOR COMMERCIAL/INVESTMENT SALES ASSOCIATES

Dear _____:

    Mr. _____, from _____ Commercial Department, mentioned the following points at last week's Board Meeting. Before showing a property he said you must be knowledgeable. To do this you must be able to answer the following:

1. What is the accessibility of the property?
2. How is the road system in _____?
3. What is the zoning?
4. If the land is vacant, what utilities are available?
5. What is the "master plan" in the area, zoning-wise?
6. How does this property compare to other similar properties in the area?
7. What would the building costs be?
8. How much does the purchaser have to spend?
9. Is this property listed with other brokers?
10. What is the condition of the money market?
11. What is the purchaser's business?
12. What about Options, Leases, Purchase Agreements?

    Please remember these points when you are analyzing Commercial/Investment property.

                                         Sincerely,

13-8 A REAL ESTATE BASICS TEST

Dear _____:

Can you pass the Real Estate Basics Test?

REAL ESTATE BASICS TEST

1. Can I do my thing in real estate—the basics of the business?
2. Can I contact four people per day? (and ask them to remember me for a favor—I need help in securing sellers?)
3. Can I spend a meaningful 55 hours a week on real estate and make myself, my family and my associates happy?
4. Can I be proud to say I am associated with the most up-to-date and fairest real estate firm in the city?
5. Can I remember that the name of the game in real estate is listings?
6. Can I use my creative mind to secure both sellers and buyers?
7. Can I convince my selling and purchasing clientele that the state's economy is healthy?
   a. Mortgage money is available
   b. There is a pent-up demand for housing
8. Can I develop a Positive Mental Attitude toward the real estate profession?
9. Can I get involved in some activity that will help my community?
10. Can I develop a Win/Win philosophy toward my fellow associates and the company?
11. Can I develop the following saying about my purchasing clientele—Show Somebody Something Somewhere each day?
12. Can I keep an up-to-date file on my friends, acquaintances, past sellers, past purchasers, present prospective sellers, present prospective purchasers, etc?
13. Can I contact owners, friends and acquaintances to secure listings? Can I follow up on expired listings?

14. Can I develop a listing farm?
15. Can I work our own listings, MLS, read the paper and drive areas to secure homes for purchasers?
16. Can I remember that real estate is a number and people business? That contacts are contracts?
17. Can I remember that if I have nothing to do in real estate, then I am doing nothing?
18. Can I remember that this profession requires much hard work? It can be aptly defined as one of the highest paying, hardest working professions or one of the least paying, least working professions.
19. Can I be honest with myself and ask for help if I am having trouble doing the basics in real estate?
20. Can I be honest mainly with myself and with my company? If I cannot do these basics, can I be straightforward and tell my company that I can't?

We will discuss these items at Thursday's sales meeting.

Sincerely,

13-9 POINTS TO COVER WITH SELLERS

Dear _____:

In order for each of you to be more professional and to make your job easier, we recommend that the following items be covered with every selling client:

1. Because of the many intangible things that affect the value of real property, it is not possible to establish the exact fair market value of a home. Therefore, recommend that the listing price be slightly in excess of the bracket given as the estimated selling price.
2. Buyers must select the home of their choice by comparison. Therefore, use the comparative market analysis approach because it has proven to be very successful in pricing property.
3. Pricing the property correctly is of importance because: Make the seller aware of the following:
   a. Homes that are on the market for too long a time are often more difficult to sell.
   b. Many salesmen lose enthusiasm after receiving a number of unfavorable reactions.
   c. Overpricing reduces the response from advertising.
   d. The property fails to compete with other properties on the market.
   e. Buyers expect more at a higher price and failing to find all they had hoped for can seldom become interested again, even at a reduced price.
   f. When a property does not sell after proper exposure to the market for a reasonable period of time, price is usually the problem.
4. Usually our best buyers are the ones already on our books because they have looked, compared, investigated the area and are familiar with and conditioned to local prices. Many times these buyers have been waiting for a definite type of property in a certain location. These buyers will be the first to

inspect the property and their offer may be the best offer obtainable.

5. We strongly recommend the use of the "For Sale" sign. Should a buyer come to the door, they should be referred to our office.

6. There are several types of financing available for homes today and it may be necessary for the seller to pay LOAN DIS- COUNT POINTS to attract a qualified buyer.

7. Keep the seller advised of our activity and welcome any suggestions as to how we can improve our service.

8. Do not become discouraged if the property does not sell quickly. There is a right buyer for every home, and finding this buyer sometimes takes a little time.

9. Make every effort to screen the buyers to determine their capabilities and qualifications prior to showing the property.

10. Since there will be many occasions when no one will be at home, we should be given a key to enable us to put up a lock box so that prospective buyers may inspect the property.

11. If at any time the seller has any questions concerning the progress being made on the sale, please have them contact our office.

Thank you. We appreciate your cooperation.

Sincerely,

13-10 ELEVEN BEAUTIFUL QUESTIONS

Dear _____:

To help you obtain good, saleable listings, you should ask yourself the following questions. You should have at least nine affirmative answers.

Qualification of the exclusive

1. Is it imperative that the owners sell?   yes no
2. Is this home comparable in value to others on the   yes no
   block?
3. Were the owners cooperative?   yes no
4. Will the owners permit a "For Sale" sign?   yes no
5. Is the market such that a favorable mortgage can be   yes no
   obtained?
6. Will the term of the exclusive be four months or   yes no
   longer?
7. Does the property possess the usual characteristics   yes no
   permitting merchandising under an exclusive
   agreement? (Unusual properties require longer to
   sell, for example, 2 bedrooms/2 story, large older
   property, deluxe property, poor location, delayed
   possession, etc.)
8. Do you think you have a reasonably good chance   yes no
   of selling the property during the term of the exclusive?
9. Are you willing to be personally responsible to the   yes no
   owners during the term of the exclusive, to keep
   them advised of our activity including buyer reactions, counsel with them as to price, etc.?
10. Have you made a complete analysis of the prop-   yes no
    erty?

11. Did at least 4 sales associates accompany you in   yes no
    looking at the property?

    I am sure you will find these very beneficial in selling the
seller—the name of the real estate game.

Sincerely,

13-11   A NEW CONCEPT: FRANCHISING

Dear _____:

We are very happy to announce to our entire staff that we are going to be on the _____ team. This is a national franchise and it will provide both you and us with the latest and most up-to-date methods in marketing property.

This does not take away from our independent business system, but adds to it. This system will provide us with the big image; yet, allows us to provide the personal service that all small businesses can and should provide for their clients.

I want to mention some of the distinct advantages of this program:

1. A national image
2. Mass advertising
3. Professional know-how in training
4. An excellent referral program
5. Recruiting program to obtain the highest caliber associates.

We have always strived to bring to our associates the finest tools and facilities available to them. This will be an excellent motivational and technique program for all of you. It will provide for you, if you will use the tools and services, the ability to be the best associate in the real estate profession.

We will discuss this program in more detail at future sales meetings.

Sincerely,

13-12 A BONUS PLAN FOR SALES AGENTS

Dear _____:

We are very pleased to announce that in addition to our present attractive commission schedule, we are now incorporating a bonus arrangement that will be within the grasp of all of our associates.

The arrangement will be based on commission dollars earned. It will be as follows:

Commission Dollars Earned		Percent added to basic sales commission
$10,000–$11,999	—	2%
$12,000–$13,999	—	Additional 2%
$14,000–$15,999	—	Additional 2%
$16,000–$17,999	—	Additional 2%
$18,000 +	—	Additional 2%

This will allow the top producer to earn a top commission at 65% once he or she has reached $18,000 and above in commissions paid in any calendar year.

We appreciate all the members of our staff, and we feel this will be an added incentive for the top professionals.

Sincerely,

13-13   ENCOURAGING ASSOCIATES TO ATTEND BREAKFAST MEETING

Dear _____:

How would you like to know methods of listing property that will give you a distinct advantage over your competitors?

We have studied each of the following three methods carefully. They are practical and easy. They do require some time, but you will have much more confidence when approaching an owner for a listing.

These three methods will be discussed at our quarterly breakfast next week:

1. Marshall and Swift
2. Competitive Market Analysis
3. Square footage average sale price for an area.

We will see you next week. Please be sure to attend this very rewarding meeting.

Sincerely,

13-14   A CONVENTION TRIP AS A SALES CONTEST PRIZE

Dear _____:

Everyone is set to begin the New Year with a bang, and we want to help!

So, in addition to our fine commission schedule and our attractive bonus plan, we are going to provide to any sales associate who exceeds $1,500,000 in sales and/or listings sold a free, all-expense paid trip for the associate and his or her spouse to the national convention in Las Vegas in November.

Come Monday to our sales meeting and hear more about the exciting news!

Sincerely,

Chapter 14

Letters That Can Settle Disputes Quickly and Effectively

The quicker real estate disputes can be settled, the better. One way to handle them quickly and effectively is through letters such as the 14 models in this chapter. . . .

14-1   EXPLAINING A TRANSACTION TO A LAND CONTRACT HOLDER

Dear _____:

There seems to be some confusion on your part about the rights of a purchaser buying on a land contract from you. Even if you are the holder of the present land contract for my seller, my seller has the right to sell the property on a new land contract to the new purchaser. The seller must continue to make payments to you, but he can also sell using this method.

I have tried to reach you for three days with no success. The purchaser I have is willing and able to assume the present land contract that you hold. He is also willing to reduce the period of the loan to 15 years instead of 20 years. This would mean approximately $16.00 more per month on the total payment.

If you would like to carry the land contract with this increase, please let me know where I can obtain the abstract. Please let me know by Friday morning, March 12.

If I do not hear from you by Friday morning, we will proceed with Mr. & Mrs. _____ carrying a new land contract. You will continue to receive the monthly payments from them. Evidence of good title will be shown by title insurance instead of an abstract. (Our purchase agreement permits good title to be shown either by an abstract or title insurance.)

This purchaser is excellent and the sale would afford you a good income. Mr. & Mrs. _____ have employed me to sell this property, and I owe them and the purchaser an obligation to close this transaction.

If you have any questions, please call me. Thank you.

Sincerely,

14-2 MODEL LETTER FOR DEALING WITH A PROBLEM INVOLVING ANOTHER BROKER

Dear _____:

    A problem has developed and I would like to call your attention to it. Your sales people are constantly besieging us and our sales people for information concerning our listings and sales. It has reached the point where it is disrupting our sales people and our office operations. We don't mind giving out data on our listings occasionally when you have a buyer you are actively working with or if you are trying to get a listing. But if you are seeking information just to complete your files that is a different story.

    I would like to suggest you join the _____ Board of Realtors and the Multiple Listing Service and then you would receive all the data on our listings and sales as well as those of many other companies.

    In any event, I would like to request that you instruct your people to call our company only when they have a bona fide client looking for a home or are trying to list a specific home. This is the procedure we expect our people to follow, and it does lead to a feeling of co-operation from other people in the business.

                                 Sincerely,

14-3 BRINGING A PROBLEM TO ANOTHER BROKER'S ATTENTION

Dear _____:

I am not going to go into detail in this letter, because I would like to have the right to come to the M.L.S. Board meeting to explain this situation fully.

The matter I am concerned about is that a member of the Multiple Listing Service has taken an exclusive listing on the above-mentioned property instead of an exclusive right-to-sell listing. This is the first one I have been aware of in my 11 years with the Board. It causes me great concern. If this practice is permitted to continue, we are going to be on a merry-go-round and we'll never have any protection.

Because this is the first case I am aware of, I do not want any severe action taken against the firm. But I do believe a strong reprimand is in order.

Thank you for your time and please advise me when I can come to your meeting.

Sincerely yours,

14-4   MODEL LETTER DETAILING A POSSIBLE BREACH OF ETHICS

Dear _____:

This is a letter I do not like to write, but I would want to know this information if the shoe were on the other foot. This concerns a sales associate of yours, Mr. _____ _____. Mr. _____ brought an offer to my home on Monday, July 23, on a lot listing of mine, multiple # _____ An answer was to be given to Mr. _____'s client by 7:00 PM on July 24.

I saw my seller at 2:00 PM on July 24th and obtained an accepted offer from her. While I was visiting with my client, she mentioned that Mr. _____ had called her direct. At 4:00 PM on July 24th I called Mr. _____ to tell him that the offer was accepted and that he could pick up the signed accep-tance. He was not in, so I left this message with another sales associate. Mr. _____ returned my call and said that he would pick up the contract on July 25, and leave the earnest deposit. This he did.

I was very confused about why Mr. _____ con-tacted my client without my knowledge. In visiting with him this morning, July 25, to see when the purchaser desired to close, I asked him why he had contacted my seller. Mr. _____ said that he had called our office and that no one there knew about the listing. I am afraid he is confused about this. I have personally checked with each of our associates and no one ever talked to him about this lot.

I also mentioned to Mr. _____ that this listing was current in Multiple, and he could have called me personally if he couldn't obtain the information. He had no answer for this. He only said that he could get no information, which is totally false. He said that he felt his next step was to call the owner. I asked him again why he didn't call me—my name appears quite plainly on the listing form. I mentioned to him that the listing was secured on May 2, _____, and that it would expire on August 2, _____. I also mentioned that on June 5, _____ we sent a change through—this appeared on the July 18 and 19th, _____ Status Report.

I don't think he called our office and obviously he didn't look at the current weekly sheet.

We have a record for cooperation and this unethical conduct disturbs me. If this happens again, I will carry it to the Grievance Committee.

In this case I feel calling him and writing you is the best solution.

Thank you, _____, and a reply will be appreciated.

                              Sincerely,

14-5 TAKING A STRONG STAND WITH AN UNHAPPY CLIENT

Dear _____:

I want to thank you for allowing our firm to sell your house.

There seemed to be some dissatisfaction on your part with our service and this certainly is not what we want. We pride ourselves in giving the best real estate service available in _____, and we feel that we do. I am sorry if you feel differently.

The areas that were brought to my attention were three: advertising, abstracting, and holding a house on the market without selling it.

As far as advertising is concerned, there are as many ideas as there are advertising agencies. But there are also some basic rules that we follow.

1. The size of the ad is insignificant if the desired message comes across. Veteran advertising agencies stand fast concerning this rule. Many companies have large signs and small house ads—this is only to promote the company image. We don't subscribe to promoting the company image alone, but rather subscribe to the idea of promoting the big feature of a house. We promoted the _____ area in advertising your house.
2. Only one ad out of 24 sells the particular house advertised. The purpose of the ad is to get the phone to ring, and thus put the sales person to work to sell the house.

The second item pertained to abstracting. We use abstracting companies, as all Realtors do, to pick up, bring up to date, and deliver to attorneys and mortgage companies. At times, there are delays because of the volume of business being done in a given time period.

The third item pertained to a company "just tying up a property." All of our sales associates, myself included, work on a commission basis, and we want to sell a property as quickly as possible and for the highest market price attainable for the client. This is why we use the most advanced competitive market analysis form when listing properties. To my knowledge we are the only company in _____ that uses an advanced form of this kind.

I am sorry you feel the way you do, but I will never back away from a problem. That's why I am writing this letter. We want to satisfy all of our clients, and it hurts when someone says we don't provide outstanding real estate service.

I am enclosing a house plaque for your new _____. Just fill out the certificate the way you wish it to read and send it to the address mentioned.

I wish you many happy years in your new home.

Sincerely,

14-6 LETTER TO A SELLER WHO REMOVED LISTED ITEMS

Dear _____:

    I certainly hope you enjoy your new home in _____.

    I received a call Saturday morning from Mrs. _____, the new owner, and she was concerned about the two stereo speakers and the air conditioner that were missing. According to the contract these items are hers and should have been left in the house.

    She is unhappy and I would like to hear any suggestions you might have on replacing these items. I certainly dislike writing this type of letter, but legally you are responsible for replacing them.

    Also she was upset that she was faced with a considerable amount of cleaning. I had informed _____ of _____ Realty of your call concerning your inability to have the house cleaned. Apparently this was not relayed to her in an appropriate manner.

    Please let me know what you think.

                               Your friend,

14-7 REQUESTING REIMBURSEMENT FOR FAULTY EQUIPMENT

Dear _____:

Mr. & Mrs. _____ have sent us a bill for $137.00 for a new hot water heater, and $35.00 for installation. They purchased the water heater wholesale from _____ Company. They had the heater installed on March 27, 19___.

The old heater was leaking at the time they took possession of the home and was not in working condition per the contract. The exact phrase in the contract is as follows:

> Seller agrees to maintain, until delivery of posses-
> sion, the heating, air conditioning, water heater,
> sewer, plumbing and electrical systems and any
> built-in appliances in working condition.

The _____'s had other problems develop with the home, but recognize they did not buy a brand new home and some problems are to be expected.

Please remit the $172.00. As I said before, this is a bill you are legally responsible for.

Sincerely,

14-8 SETTLING A MINOR DISPUTE BETWEEN BUYER AND SELLER

Dear _____:

I was sorry to hear of your displeasure and we certainly don't want any of our clients to be unhappy. I am quite aware that the seller did promise to keep the lawn maintained until closing. Unfortunately, she had serious domestic and personal problems.

It could be, I am sure, an unending debate as to whose responsibility it is to maintain a lawn. In most cases, the seller would care for such items. We have had a different situation here, and I hope the enclosed check will assist you with this problem.

Thank you again for your confidence in me and our firm. I certainly wish you years of happiness in your new home.

Sincerely,

14-9 A MODEL EXPLANATION OF THE SALES PROCESS TO AN UNHAPPY SELLER

Dear _____:

Please allow me to introduce myself. I am _____ _____, the gentleman who sold your property at 81st & _____ Street in _____, _____.

Every aspect of the transaction was going along smoothly until this afternoon. I received a phone call from Mr. B_____, the executor of the estate. He was very angry after receiving the contract signed by you and notarized. I am still completely puzzled by his anger and accusations. He told me that he never authorized the $39,000 contract and the Mr. C_____, the attorney for the estate, the buyer, the veteran's administration, and myself were collaborating to take all we could from the estate. This was very shocking to me, because I am a Realtor who is governed by a Code of Ethics. I would never engage in this type of transaction.

I am sure that this matter is one of faulty communications and not a matter of malice on either side. Mr. B_____ is a fine individual and our relationship was cordial until his call this afternoon. I told him this evening in a telephone conversation that our one goal was to remain the same—a mutually satisfactory closing of the estate for all parties concerned.

Please let me relate to you the complete transaction from the start. After showing the property to many prospects without obtaining an offer (because they said the price was too high), I obtained an offer from Mr. and Mrs. _____. The offer was for $39,500 on a Veteran's Administration loan. I contacted Mr. B_____ and he signed this agreement. I was not aware at the time that he did not have the authority to sign it. I told him at the time of his signature that the house could not sell for any more than what the Veteran's Administration appraised it for. We ran the V. A. Appraisal and it came back at $39,000 for 30 years, with the stipulation that the sewer, if in, would be paid and connected by the seller. (They based their appraisal on the basic of a sewer in the street and connected.) I immediately called Mr. B_____ with this information. He said he would check with you for your answer. He called me back at 1:00 PM Saturday afternoon and told me that you had accepted this.

Because of the change of price, it necessitated a new contract. Because I had been given the go-ahead by Mr. B_____, I contacted Mr. C_____ to keep him abreast of the transaction. He asked me if Mr. B_____ was aware of the happenings, and I told him yes. I also asked Mr. C_____ if I should have Mr. B_____ sign the second purchase agreement, and he said this would not be a legal contract, because the will of the estate did not provide for the executor to have the right to sign the contract. So, naturally I sent the contract to Mr. C_____ to have forwarded to you for your signature. I certainly did not mean to avoid Mr. B_____.

I received your signed contract Friday and sent a copy of it to the Veteran's Administration. (The Veteran's Administration requires that the proper person must sign the contract and they did not dispute your signing of it.) I say again that I was advised to send the new contract to Mr. C_____ and he would forward it to you.

As to the merits of the sale price of the house, there is no question in my mind that this $39,000 figure is the marketable price. I am a Realtor in the field everyday, and am sure my judgment is correct. I had another party who was thinking of offering $36,500 cash, but Mr. & Mrs. _____ offered first. Even with the expenses to the estate for sewer, mortgage company discount points charged the seller for Veteran Administration loans, and the real estate service fee, the estate is still coming out better than if it were a $36,500 cash offer. The approximate costs to the estate which I explained to Mr. B_____ will be:

Sewer Assessment	$630.00
Mortgage Co. Discount	1,170.00
Sewer Connection	329.00
Real Estate fee	2,730.00
	$4,859.00

Subtract this from $39,000 and it is approximately 34,141 net.

Don't be shocked by the sewer bill. The septic tank was completely unworkable, and I have a signed statement to this effect. So it was either a sewer or a new septic tank. The septic tank was to cost $400.00.

I am sorry and stunned at this development. I am sure that Mr. B_____ was hurt because we did not have him sign the second purchase agreement. But as I have explained before, this was not done intentionally. I only followed the advice of the lawyer for the estate. I had informed Mr. B_____ of the change and he called you for your approval. I felt that I should also keep the attorney posted.

I know that Mr. B_____ is acting in good faith, and I can reassure you that I am. I feel that I have handled the transaction in a businesslike manner and am entitled to my service fee if the transaction closes according to the original contract I received in the mail Friday.

Let's hope this misunderstanding is cleared up, and that we can close as of the 15th of August. Please inform me of what I should do. Call me if necessary. Thank you.

Sincerely,

14-10 LETTER TO AGENT CONCERNING MECHANICAL PROBLEMS

Dear _____:

    Since I could not reach you by phone, I am writing to you. Mr. & Mrs. _____ asked me to get in touch with you to advise you that the air conditioner is not working in the house they purchased from you and Mr. _____ at _____ Street. They had an estimate made by a licensed Air Conditioning Company, which I am enclosing. Chances are you have a subcontract working for you who can make the repairs.

    According to the purchase contract, dated June 26, the seller agreed to keep the air conditioner in working condition until delivery of possession. Therefore, please forward your check for the amount of the estimate, or let us know when repairs will be made. Thank you very much.

                               Sincerely,

14-11   DEALING WITH A HESITANT SELLER

Dear _____:

     This letter is to advise you that our purchaser is ready and able to close the transaction on your home according to the provisions of the contract.

     We must have the abstract immediately in order to have evidence of good title. The abstract must be brought up to date and sent to the purchaser's attorney for his examination.

     Please let me know when I can obtain the abstract or have your attorney call me concerning your problem. We would like to move ahead quickly.

                    Sincerely,

14-12   LETTER AND MODEL RELEASE FORM TO BUYERS WHO ARE BACKING OUT

Dear _____:

     I must have this release signed by both you and your wife to enable us to place the home back on the market. Please read this release, authorize it, have it notarized and return it to me.

     I am very sorry you had a change of heart because I know you would have enjoyed this home. Situations like this are never easy. The agreement is attached to this letter.

                    Sincerely,

RELEASE

_____, _____
_____ _____ COMPANY, Agent
On   March   17,   _____,   WE,   _____
_____ AND _____ _____, agreed
to   purchase   property   located   at   _____   North
_____ Street, _____, _____, from
_____ __ _____ and _____ __
_____, the owners and paid Earnest Money in the
amount of $1,000.00 to _____ _____ Com-
pany, Agent for _____ __ _____ and
_____ __ _____. We hereby acknowledge
receipt of our earnest money deposit in the amount of $1,000 less
expense of credit report of $7.50 and extension of abstract of
$20.00. We have refused to consummate purchase of said property
and therefore authorize _____ _____ Com-
pany to put said property back on the market.

_____

_____

STATE OF _____

COUNTY OF _____ SS

Subscribed and sworn to before me this _____ day of
_____, 19__.

_____
                                    Notary Public

My Commission expires _____

14-13   SELLER'S AUTHORIZATION TO RETURN EARNEST DEPOSIT

Dear _____:

     I am enclosing an agreement authorizing us to return the earnest deposit to the prospective purchaser. This must be acknowledged, notarized, and returned to me in order for our company to place your home back on the market.

     Let's forget this unhappy situation and strive to obtain another satisfactory offer on your home.

     Thank you for your continued confidence in our firm.

Sincerely,

RELEASE

On March 17, 19___, We, _____ ___ _____
and _____ ___ _____ agreed to sell property
located at _____ North _____ Street,
_____, _____, to _____
_____ and _____ _____, on which
they paid an earnest money deposit of $1,000.00 to
_____ _____ Company, as agents for
_____ ___ _____ and _____ ___
_____. I, _____ ___ _____ and
_____ ___ _____, hereby authorize
_____ _____ Company as my agent, to re-
fund earnest money in the amount of $1,000 less expense of credit
report of $7.50 and extension of abstract of $20.00 to
_____ _____ and _____
_____.

_____

_____

STATE OF _____
COUNTY OF _____ SS

Subscribed and sworn to before me this _____ day of
_____, 19___

_____
                              Notary Public

My commission expires _____

14-14   CONVINCING AN ATTORNEY TO GIVE A NET LISTING

Dear _____:

We would like to be your client's Realtor. You can be assured that we will work hard at getting the best price possible for him.

However, it is not our policy to take a new listing. It would appear a net listing is the ideal situation for a seller, but we submit that it is not.

We feel property listed with us should be fully exposed by advertising to Multiple Listing. We believe if we sell your property or another broker sells it, we are entitled to our usual commission; no more and no less.

We take the time to analyze each property we list to determine what a normal buyer should pay for it. Your client's property is not an easy piece of property to analyze because of the unusual bedroom arrangement and because people are reacting to oil heat because of the energy crisis.

We have taken those factors into consideration. We have put in report form that we feel the property should sell for $36,000. We recommended that the property be listed slightly in excess of that at $37,500. We have further submitted an approximate net sheet showing what your clients would net. Also sent to you was our usual Listing Agreement. This is far more than most companies would have done voluntarily at this point, but it is an example of our belief in going the extra mile. If we fail to bring you an offer of $37,500 or one for less that is acceptable to your clients, they owe us nothing. All our advertising and time spent on your client's property will be absolutely free. We must produce to be paid and we feel our services are reasonably priced at 7% of the gross selling price.

We would like to go to work for you, but under the regular listing arrangement using the standard listing agreement used by the _____ Real Estate Board and Multiple Listing Service.

We hope you understand our position and will agree to put us to work.

Sincerely,